"Hardside love is doing what's best for another person *regardless of the cost*. It's the strength a mother needs to stand up to a defiant two-year-old. It's the courage of a father who risks his relationship with his daughter to point out how far she's wandered. . . . But hardside love is incomplete by itself.

"Softside love is a tenderness. . . . It's the sympathy of a father who sits with an arm around his daughter as she cries over a lost boyfriend, and doesn't even hint at a lecture. It's also the wisdom to ask 'Will you forgive me?' or to say 'I was wrong,' especially to our children. . . .

"It's essential that we learn to balance love's two sides if we want to communicate the deepest, most meaningful kind of love."

—Gary Smalley and John Trent

GARY SMALLEY, president of Today's Family in Phoenix, holds a bachelor's degree in psychology and has a master's degree from Bethel Seminary in St. Paul, Minnesota. His previous bestselling books include *If Only He Knew, For Better or For Best* and *The Key to Your Child's Heart*. Gary and his wife, Norma, are the parents of three children, Kari, Greg and Michael.

JOHN TRENT, vice president of Today's Family, has a Ph.D. in marriage and family counseling and holds a master's degree from Dallas Theological Seminary. He coauthored with Gary the bestselling books *The Blessing, The Gift of Honor, The Language of Love, Love Is a Decision* and *The Two Sides of Love*. He lives in Phoenix with his wife, Cynthia, and daughters, Kari Lorraine and Laura Catherine.

S0-CAA-105

Books by Gary Smalley & John Trent, Ph.D.

The Blessing
The Gift of Honor
The Language of Love
Love Is a Decision
The Two Sides of Love

Published by POCKET BOOKS

The
TWO SIDES
of
LOVE

GARY SMALLEY &
JOHN TRENT, PH.D.

POCKET BOOKS

New York   London   Toronto   Sydney   Tokyo   Singapore

Unless otherwise noted, Scripture quotations are from the Holy Bible, New International Version, copyright © 1973, 1978, 1984 by the International Bible Society.

People's names and certain details of case studies mentioned in this book have been changed to protect the privacy of the individuals involved. However, we have attempted to convey the essence of the experience and the underlying principles as accurately as possible.

POCKET BOOKS, a division of Simon & Schuster Inc. 1230 Avenue of the Americas, New York, NY 10020

Copyright © 1990, 1992 by Gary Smalley and John Trent, Ph.D.

Published by arrangement with Word Inc.

ISBN: 0-671-75053-4

First Pocket Books printing August 1993

10 9 8 7 6 5 4 3 2 1

POCKET and colophon are registered trademarks of Simon & Schuster Inc.

Cover design by Darlene Barbaria

Printed in the U.S.A.

We lovingly dedicate this book to our wives,
Norma and Cynthia,
each an expert at giving both sides of love;
and to George and Liz Toles, faithful friends,
consistent encouragers and godly examples to us
over the years.

Contents

CONTENTS

The
TWO SIDES
of
LOVE

1

Discovering Love's Two Sides

Darrell stood outside the local pizza parlor, hesitating before he opened the door. He shook his head as if to clear away his last-minute doubts about this meeting. Finally, with a sigh, he forced aside his fear, pushed open the door, and walked into his son's favorite restaurant.

He dreaded this meeting so much that it took all his emotional strength just to walk inside instead of turning away. Little did he know that within a few hours, he would experience one of the most positive events of his life.

Darrell had come to meet his seventeen-year-old son, Charles. Though Darrell loved Charles deeply, he also knew that of his two boys, Charles was the most different from him.

With his older son, Larry, communication was never a struggle. They acted and thought so much alike that they didn't need to talk much. They just did things together, like hunting or working on their cars. Darrell had always treated Larry as he did the men at his construction sites—rough. And Larry had always responded well to—even thrived on—that kind of treatment.

But Charles was a different case. Darrell could tell early on that Charles was much more sensitive than Larry. Each time Darrell blasted this son to motivate him like his older brother, Darrell could hear an alarm going off deep inside himself.

Darrell had received major doses of discipline and distance in his life—the hard side of love—but only a scant spoonful of warmth and acceptance—love's soft side. And what little he had been given, he had also measured out to his sons.

It's my job to put clothes on their backs and food on the table; it's their mother's job to make them feel loved, he told himself over and over. But he couldn't quite convince himself that that was all there was to being a father. Darrell knew how deeply he had been hurt by his own dad. And he had seen that same hurt in Charles's eyes a hundred times.

Darrell knew what a major part of the problem was. Charles had expected—almost demanded—a close relationship with him over the years. It wasn't enough that they go hunting together. Charles wanted to talk while they were on the trip—even while they were hunting!

Only recently had Darrell realized that the sole reason he and Charles were getting along at the moment was that his son had quit talking to him altogether! Just as Darrell had done as a teenager with his own tough father, Charles had withdrawn to a safe distance and was doing his best to stay out of his dad's way.

Like many of us, Darrell had been on the run from close relationships. For years, his wife and son had been pursuing him. And for as many years, he'd been running away from them, trying to keep a "comfortable" distance between them.

Then one day Darrell got a clear look at himself during a men's retreat at his church, and the running stopped.

That day at the retreat, he came face to face with the fact that there are two sides of love. Like many men, he had become an expert on its hard side. He could hand out the spankings, but not reach out to hug his son. In a heartbeat he could call down a mistake Charles made, but words of encouragement came up only on a holiday or birthday—if then.

At that men's retreat, Darrell learned that as important as a mother's love is, children need more. They desperately need their father's whole-hearted love as well.

Darrell was a strong man, both emotionally and physically. Yet as tough as he fancied himself, just one question the speaker asked pierced through to his heart: "When was the last time you put your arms around your son and told him face to face that you love him?"

Darrell couldn't think of a "last time." In fact, he couldn't think of a first time.

He listened as the speaker told him that genuine love has two sides, not just one. Instantly he realized he had been loving Charles only half-heartedly and that his son needed both sides of love *from the same person.*

What Charles needed most in a father was a real man who could show him how to love a wife and family wholeheartedly, not an insecure man who had to hand off all the warm and loving actions to his wife. Darrell had spent years hardsiding his son to gain his respect; what he had gained instead was his fear and resentment. And it was this realization that caused Darrell to talk his son into meeting him at the local pizza restaurant after football practice one afternoon.

"Hi, Dad," Charles said, shaking hands with his father, who had just walked in. Charles was six foot two and was used to looking down when he greeted people. But he was looking up to meet his dad's eyes. And although Darrell had turned fifty-one that same month, he had none of the middle-age spread that most men his age carry. Instead, he still possessed the athletic build that had made him a star on his high school football team.

Charles and his father were the kind of people

that "all you can eat" restaurant managers hate to see walk in the door. That evening they kept their waitress running back and forth as they devoured three baskets of bread sticks and nearly as many pizzas. As their dinner progressed from appetizers to the main course, their conversation moved from small talk to the serious matter Darrell wanted to discuss.

"Charles," Darrell said, adjusting his glasses and looking down slightly as he spoke, "I've been doing a lot of thinking lately. It's been hitting me hard that this is your last summer at home. You'll be leaving for college soon. And along with the bags of clothing you'll be packing, you'll also be taking emotional bags that, for good or bad, *I've* helped you pack over the years."

Charles was normally the family comedian, but this time, instead of trying to "lighten up" the conversation, he sat quietly. It wasn't like his father to talk about their relationship. In fact, it wasn't like him to talk about *anything* serious. That's why he was all ears as he listened to his father.

"Son, I'd like to ask you to do something. Think back as far as you can—back to three years old even—and remember every time I've hurt your feelings and never made things right; every time I've made you feel unloved or inadequate by something I've said or done.

"I know we're different people. I can see now that I was always pretty hard on you. Actually, I was way too tough on you most of the time. I've tried to push you into being the person I thought you should be. Now I realize I've spent very little time listening to who you really want to become.

"Feel free to share with me anything I've done that's hurt you, and all I'm going to do is listen. Then I'd like for us to talk about it, and I want to ask your forgiveness for each thing you can think of. You don't need to be packing any extra, negative baggage that I may have given you. You've got enough ahead of you over the next four years in college without that.

"I realize there's been a lot of water under the bridge—a lot of wasted years." Taking off his glasses and wiping tears from his eyes, he sighed, then looked straight at Charles. "We may be here all night," he continued, "and I'm ready for that. But first, you need to know how much I love you and how proud I am of you."

Charles had seen the words "I love you" written on birthday and Christmas cards in his father's handwriting, but this was the first time he had heard them from his father's lips. He'd learned to expect his father's hardness. Now that Dad had added softness to his love, Charles didn't know what to say.

"Dad," he stammered, "don't worry about the past. I know you love me." But at his father's insistence, he put his memory on "rewind" and let his thoughts fly back across the pictures he'd accumulated from seventeen years of being with his dad.

Slowly, as Charles grew more confident that the conversational waters really were safe, he unloaded years of hurt right at the table. There were the seasons he spent becoming an outstanding football player to please his father, when all the time he would rather have been playing soccer.

There was the subtle resentment he had always felt that no matter how hard he tried, he could never quite live up to his older brother's accomplishments. And there were the many harsh comments his father had made to motivate him but that had actually been discouraging and hurtful.

As he recounted to his father each experience, large or small, Charles could see a genuine softness and sorrow in his dad's eyes. What's more, he heard words of remorse and healing for even the smallest thing that had left a rough edge on a memory.

Nearly three hours later, the fruitful conversation finally came to an end. As Darrell reached for the check, he said, "I know this was quick notice for you to have to think back on seventeen years. So just remember, my door is always open if there's anything else I need to ask your forgiveness for."

Dinner was over, but a new relationship was just beginning for them. After eighteen years of being strangers living under the same roof, they were finally on their way to finding each other.

Not long ago, television news cameras captured thousands of people cheering as the Berlin Wall came down after dividing the city for more than twenty-five years. And that night in the restaurant, we can just imagine that angels stood all around and cheered as the first hole in an emotional wall between a father and son was blown open.

It had been a moving night and an important one for both of them. But as they stood up, Charles did something that shocked his father.

Several people looked up from tables nearby as a big, strapping football player reached out and gave his equally strong father a warm bear hug for the first time in years. With tears in their eyes, those two strong men stood there holding each other, oblivious to the stares.

What Are the Two Sides of Love?

In many ways, on the football field and in the building business, Darrell was a warrior who had conquered any challenges put before him. But for all his success, he had never won the bigger battle for his son's heart until that night. How did it happen? While Darrell was at his retreat, he discovered the same things you will in this book.

It's essential that we learn to balance love's hard and soft sides every day if we want to communicate to others the deepest, most meaningful kind of love.

It's essential that we learn to balance love's two sides if we want to communicate the deepest, most meaningful kind of love.

What do we mean by "hardside" and "softside" love, and why is it so important to understand and communicate both of them to others? While it may seem an unlikely place to look, nature provides a classic illustration of the answers to those questions.

One of the most beautiful things in all God's creation is a rose. In our culture, roses signify love, hearty congratulations or other deep emotions. Roses have been bred to capture and show off the colors of the rainbow. There's great softness in them as well. Like the tenderness of a baby's skin, velvety rose petals beg to be touched.

But God knew when He designed the rose that the very softness that makes it a thing of splendor also leaves it easy prey to those creatures that would destroy its beauty. That's why, along with the softness, He also provided the hardness of thorns. They don't detract from its beauty but protect, preserve and enhance it.

What's true in the realm of nature is also true in the world of relationships.

Hardside love is doing what's best for another person *regardless of the cost.* Held in balance, it's the ability to be consistent, to discipline, to protect, to challenge and to correct.

It's the strength a mother needs to stand up to a defiant two-year-old instead of caving in to his immature demands. It's the courage of a father who risks his relationship with his daughter to point out how far she's wandered from the Lord. It's the power an elderly husband demonstrates every day he stays and cares for the wife of his youth who is smitten with Alzheimer's disease instead of giving up and walking away.

Like the thorns on a rose, hardside love is protective. But if left to grow unchecked and never cut back to allow for healthy softside growth, it can become a thornbush instead of a rosebush. Instead of drawing people to its beauty, it can be hurtful and even cause them to move and stay away.

Hardside love is essential. But it's also incomplete by itself.

Softside love is a tenderness that grows to be the same color as unconditional love. When held in balance, it manifests characteristics like compassion, sensitivity, patience and understanding.

It's the sympathy of a father who sits with his arm around his daughter as she cries over a lost boyfriend, and the dad doesn't even hint at a lecture or an "I told you so." It's the encouragement of a mother whose cheerful card arrives at the college post office the day before her son's medical school entrance exams. And it's the kindness of a man who still calls his best friend's parents each year on the day their son died in Vietnam—just to let them know he remembers and that their son is more than a name on a wall.

Softside love takes time to understand another's feelings and listens instead of lecturing. It shows itself in the willingness to reach out and warmly touch and hug someone. It's also the wisdom to ask "Will you forgive me?" or to say "I was wrong," especially to our children.

Like hardside love, softside love can be pushed out of balance. Without a protective hard side, it can become so emotional and unstable that all the soft petals end up withered on the ground.

Is such a view of love novel? Is trying to understand and balance these two sides of love an invitation to confusion? Hardly. It's actually the very way we were always meant to love others. For it's the way the greatest lover of all time loves us—God Himself.

The Source of Love

Have you ever wondered what God is like? Isaiah the prophet gave two closely connected word pictures to the people of Judah in anticipation of their being conquered by Babylon and taken into captivity for seventy years.[1] At the end of that time, the weary refugees would experience God's presence again and finally return to the promised land. Get up on the rooftops and mountains, Isaiah told them in the first picture, because "the Sovereign Lord comes with power, and his arm rules for him" (Isa. 40:10). In Old Testament times, this signified a conquering warrior in all his strength. It was a clear picture of His hardside love.

But then we see the second picture in verse 11: "He tends His flock like a shepherd: He gathers the

11

lambs in his arms and carries them close to his heart; he gently leads those that have young." God is a caring, loving shepherd who "gently" tends to those with special needs. That was a clear picture of His softside love.

The people weren't being told that two Gods were in view—just one. But our God does have two sides to His love: a hard side that's consistent, purposeful, protective and mighty with judgment; and a soft side that's compassionate, tender, forgiving and merciful.

If we're serious about what it means to love others with our whole heart, the place to begin is by looking to the greatest lover of all time, Jesus Christ. He loved a sinful world enough to take off the mantle of heavenly power and be born in a stable. What's more, He demonstrated that love to us in that while we were still His enemies, He died for us on the cross.[2]

Jesus had the ability to give softside love to Peter, warmly saying to him after his great confession of faith, "Blessed are you, Simon son of Jonah, for this was not revealed to you by man, but by my Father in heaven."[3] Yet just a short time later, He could draw on the healthy, protective, hard side of love to say to Peter, "Get behind me, Satan! You are a stumbling block to me; you do not have in mind the things of God, but the things of men."[4]

Christ wasn't being inconsistent in His love. Neither was He on an emotional roller-coaster ride, alternately critical and caring. Rather, He was demonstrating the same two characteristics Isaiah spoke about when he described God as both sovereign Lord and a tender shepherd.

As the visible expression of the invisible God, Jesus showed us that His love was soft enough to cry at the death of a friend, to hug children and have them sit in His lap. Yet it was hard enough to confront those opposed to God's way and to "resolutely set out for Jerusalem"[5] and the cross no matter what the personal cost.

Jesus was always soft with people, yet hard on their problems.

If we want to love in a Christlike way, our love must have both hard and soft sides. Specifically, we need to remember that *He was always soft with people, yet hard on their problems.*

Jesus was soft with people like Peter, the rich young ruler and Paul. But He was consistently hard on their problems of pride, greed and hatred. He blasted the Pharisees who challenged Him, calling them white-washed graves and blind guides. Yet whenever one of these religious leaders turned to Him with a sincere faith—like Nicodemus, the rich young ruler or Joseph of Arimathea—His softside love was always there, ready to forgive, comfort, show mercy and point to the truth.

Christ used the hard side of love to confront wrong, but He also knew there are times when a person most needs softness. Under pressure from the Pharisees not to heal on the Sabbath, He rebuked their hardness of heart. He would always do what was loving, and at times that meant touching, healing and forgiving even when the Pharisees' rules forbade it.

What does this all have to do with a book on marriage, parenting and relationships?

Until we learn to love others the way God loves us—with both of love's sides—we'll never have the kind of relationships that reflect the nature of God.

As soon as Darrell, whose story opened this chapter, heard the concept, he knew he was a pro at being hardside with Charles. But when it came to expressing the soft side of love, he wasn't even on the course.

That dinner meeting with Charles was one of his first steps toward balancing the two sides of whole-hearted love. It wasn't easy, and it didn't come naturally to him. But he learned the same things you will in this book—insights that can help you to add a loving softness or a healthy hard side to your life.

As Darrell put these ideas into practice, he saw major improvements in his relationships both at home and at work. In fact, all across the country we've seen many people experience these same benefits as they've understood and applied the two sides of love. Just what did they learn that you can as well?

- *You'll soon discover a method for identifying your personal balance point.* Is your love shifted to one extreme or the other? Do you find yourself at the North Pole and your spouse at the South when it comes to being hard and soft? As your spouse gets harder, do you find yourself getting softer (or vice versa) to bring some kind of balance into your home?

All the warmth of love can be frozen in relationships that are out of balance, and discovering your personal balance point is the first way to begin to protect or repair a relationship.

- *You'll learn how your natural personality strengths can push you out of balance either hardside or softside.* Many books can help you discover your basic personality type, but it's not enough just to understand your natural bent. Even more important is recognizing how that natural bent can push you into an unbalanced relationship and rob you and your family of harmony and intimacy.

- *You'll see how you can identify and cut down on any unhealthy distance in your relationships.* Do you sense there's too much emotional distance in your marriage or between you and your children? Like Darrell, have you been aware of an inner alarm that's telling you, *We're not as close as we should be?*

In the chapters to come, you'll learn what causes unhealthy distance in a relationship and how applying the two sides of love can move you closer to your loved ones than ever before.

- *You'll see how "emotional freeze points" can rob us of the ability to love wholeheartedly.* In many people's lives, some past event or season has frozen them into a particular way of relating to others, blocking the flow of love's two sides. And identifying and dealing with those freeze points is crucial in building and protecting strong relationships.

- *You'll learn ten ways a person who is too soft can add a healthy hardness to his or her love, and ten ways a hardside person can become softer.* Once you understand where you are today and how your basic personality may be pushing you to an unhealthy extreme, you'll discover twenty specific ways to balance your love and strengthen the bonds between yourself and others.

Taking the First Step Toward Balance

At the retreat he attended, Darrell came face to face with himself. But that weekend wasn't simply a time to look in the mirror and go away unchanged. Darrell took the time to ask hard questions of himself and to do something that helped him discover how far out of balance he actually was.

In less than five minutes, Darrell was able to pinpoint where he was in his most important relationships, both hardside and softside—the same thing you'll be able to do in a few pages.

In just a few moments' time, he saw a new side to himself. What's more, as he began to move toward balance, he won back something of immeasurable value—his son's heart.

Perhaps you don't have a relationship on the critical list. But you can still benefit from this book, because improving your relationship skills will directly benefit your marriage, friendships, family and work setting. By learning to give and receive the two sides of love, you'll see even strong relationships grow deeper and more committed.

It all begins with your taking a few minutes to pinpoint where you are today, either hardside or softside, in the way you relate to others. And after that important first step, we want to give you a number of practical tools that can put both sides of love well within your reach.

2

How Hard or Soft Are You?

In just a few pages, you'll find a short but important survey that helps you see your own tendency toward hardness or softness. You may be surprised by what you discover about yourself.

First, however, we have a confession to make. Out of all the books we've written, either together or separately, this is the one *we've* needed the most, both personally and with our families. Let us explain.

When we first decided to write this book, we sat down with our wives, Norma and Cindy, to have them sign off on the project. We involve them in all our publishing decisions because we respect their input, and also because the long days and nights

18

that go with writing a book are not just demanding on us, but on the rest of our families as well. That's why we don't go forward with any writing project unless we're all in unity.

Normally, when the four of us sit down to talk over a book idea, it's a fun afternoon or evening of discussion. Then everyone agrees, often in writing, to go forward as a team with the project.

At least that's the way it's *supposed* to work. But when it came to discussing this book—well, we'll never forget what happened.

It was several years ago now that we first met with our wives to talk over *The Two Sides of Love*. As we had done in the past, we wrote up a short summary of the book and gave it to them in advance for their review.

Going into the meeting, we knew for certain that they'd be excited about this project. We could just see them jumping up from the table, giving us high fives, and shouting, "Go get 'em, guys!" As it turned out, things were jumping all right, but for a very different reason.

You have to picture the scene. We're on one side of the table in our conference room, grinning and talking excitedly about the need to get started writing this important book. Our wives are on the other side of the table, watching our excitement but knowing we're missing something crucial.

In a presentation worthy of any Fortune 500 company, we did our best to sell them on the central concept of this book. Finally, we grinned and leaned back in our chairs. All that was left was to hear their cheers and get their signatures on the dotted line. At least that's what we thought.

It was softside Norma who spoke up first—someone who normally avoids confrontation at all costs.

"Cindy and I have talked," she said, glancing over at her for support, "and we love the concept. We think you're right: there do seem to be two sides to love. What's more, we can see how important it is to be balanced in the way we love others. Giving only one side of love can cause real problems in a family, friendship or any other kind of meaningful relationship.

"We think it's a great idea. It's a ten. What's more, it's grounded in the Scriptures, and we think it can help a lot of people."

Up to this point, everything she'd said couldn't have sounded better. We *knew* they'd see things our way! We were ready to close the meeting and pick up the phone to call the publisher when Norma said, "But we can't sign off on this book—at least not yet."

"What?" we said in stereo, our mouths dropping open.

"You two have always told us that you only want to write books about things you've lived and practiced in your own homes, right?"

We nodded agreement, unaware of the trap we were walking into.

"Both of you are practicing a lot of what you've said you want to put in the book. But before you write it, there are a few things we feel you still need to finish.

"When it comes to marriage, you've both got the hard side of love down pat. But while the soft side is certainly there, too, we'd like to see it even more often with the two of us. What's more, even though you're both good fathers, we'd still like to see a better balance with the children at times."

I (John) looked to Cindy, hoping to hear her say to Norma, "Oh, that's not true about John! *Gary,* maybe, but not *my* husband." Instead, all I got was seasick from watching her head bob up and down in agreement.

They were right, of course. (How often they are!) But still we asked for examples. . . . We shouldn't have.

Fit to Be Tied

"John," Cindy said in her kindest voice, "I never doubt your commitment to Kari and me. But you're not quite balanced when it comes to giving us both sides of love."

"What do you mean?" I asked in genuine puzzlement.

"Sometimes you give me one side of love and Kari the other. What we really need is what you want to write about—the two sides of love."

"Give us a 'for instance,'" Gary said with a grin as I shot him a look that said, "Just wait till it's *your* turn."

"Take what happened after your last trip," Cindy

offered. "Can you remember how you greeted me when you first walked in the door after being gone three days?"

Unfortunately, I did remember. The day I left on that trip, she had been very busy with our daughter and had forgotten to pick up some dry cleaning I was going to take with me. Naturally, I didn't think of the cleaning, either, until I was already in the air and realized I didn't have my only sportcoat along.

When did I let her know how inconvenienced I had been because she didn't pick up the dry cleaning as we had agreed? Regrettably, I chose to tell her as soon as I'd walked into the house.

"John," she said now, "you don't have any trouble giving me the hard side of love. But after you'd been away for several days, what I needed when I met you at the door was your soft side—a hug and a warm hello—not a lecture about forgetting your cleaning."

Right there in the middle of the conference room, I started looking for a hole to crawl into. And after she told me her next concern, I was ready to cover over the hole!

"That's not all," she continued. "There have been a number of times recently when you've given Kari just one side of love as well. Remember the other night with the dental floss?"

Once again, she had brought to mind something I was far more eager to forget.

"You do a great job of giving Kari the softside love she needs," she said. "But when it comes to being hard with her when she needs it, like following through on family rules . . ."

Cindy didn't have to say anything more. I knew exactly what she meant. We have a family rule that no one can pull out more than three feet of dental floss a night. The rule came into existence after Kari had pulled out seventy-five yards of the stuff one day.

Everyone in the family was clear on the rule— but I wasn't enforcing it. When it was my turn to help Kari get ready for bed, I would "look the other way" as she pulled out ten or twelve feet of the bubble-gum-flavored string.

After all, I reasoned, it was cute watching her do it . . . and she would only be four once . . . and it was such a *small* rule. But it was beginning to have a much larger effect on my wife and daughter's relationship than I had ever dreamed.

"The other night, when you were on your trip," Cindy said, "Kari started pulling out yards of dental floss. When I told her she could only pull out three feet, immediately her lip went out and she told me in a defiant voice, *'Daddy* lets me do it!'

"'Oh he does, does he?' I said.

"'That's right. And you know what? I like Daddy better than you, Mommy.'

"'Why's that?' I asked.

"'*Because Daddy doesn't make me follow the rules.*'"

Cindy paused for what seemed like an hour before she continued, "John, Kari knows you love her, but there are times when you're too soft with her. When I keep the family rules and you don't, you make me look rock hard, but it's really you who's out of balance!"

She leaned over, took my hand, and said with a smile, "Honey, I'm not trying to be too hardside with you. I wouldn't trade you for any other husband or father in the world.

"But come to think of it," she added with a twinkle in her eye, "maybe it *is* a good idea for you to write this book. If it will help you learn how to be softer with me at times and harder with Kari, I'm ready to say yes today!"

My frown changed immediately to a grin when I realized Cindy was finished. *It's your turn now, Gary,* I figured. I was right.

"Gary," Norma said gently, "do you think you need more balance in the two sides of love?"

"Who, me?" I (Gary) asked.

To jog my memory, she said, "Remember the time with Mike and the banana?"

We were living in Texas at the time and had just returned from a long trip. I had driven for hours, trying to stay awake by talking on the CB and drinking coffee (which I hate). All I could think about was getting home and crawling into bed. Finally, well after midnight, I pulled into our driveway and had everyone pile out of the car.

"Come on, kids," I said. "Everyone to bed. Right now."

Michael, who was only about five at the time,

then said the last thing I wanted to hear: "Daddy, I'm hungry. Can I eat something?"

"No way!" I said, my voice filled with frustration and the need for sleep. "We're all tired, and if you stay up and eat, everyone else will want to stay up and eat. Then it'll be another hour before we're all in bed. So go get on your pajamas, and do it now!"

"Gary," Norma said soothingly, "it's been a long trip. If he wants to eat some cereal, I'll stay up with him for a few minutes so you can go to bed."

Now I was irritated at Mike for wanting to stay up and at Norma for exposing my insensitivity. Out of pure frustration, I said, "You want something to eat, Mike? Okay!"

In a flash, I grabbed a banana off the shelf, peeled it, and shoved it toward him. Unfortunately, he moved toward me at the same time, and the banana hit him in the face *near* his mouth, but not in it.

As Mom rushed in to protect her son from the banana, chaos broke out in our home. My selfishness and lack of sensitivity had closed both my wife's and son's spirits and landed me in major trouble. I was so ashamed and upset with myself that I couldn't get to sleep that night anyway!

I asked for forgiveness from both of them right then, before we all went to bed, but it still took days for everything to thaw out. And now Norma was calling that scene back to mind.

"Gary, most of the time you're wonderful with the kids," she said. "They all know how much you love them and how proud you are of them. But occasionally—especially with Michael—you can be very critical. And when that happens, it's like you're pushing a banana into his mouth again!"

Once was enough for the banana incident. I could see exactly what she meant, and I knew that like John, I needed to give more-balanced love in my own home—and made the commitment to do so.

"I agree with Cindy," Norma added. "This is a good book idea. In fact, I'd like nothing more than to have you concentrate on adding softness to our relationship and home over the next few years." Then she said, "And when the book's done, I'll keep a copy next to the bed in case I need to get at it quickly!"

As you've obviously figured, since you're holding this book in your hands, Norma and Cindy finally agreed that we could write the book after we had been putting these concepts into practice for several months. That afternoon, they used the principles you'll learn here to help strengthen both the Smalley and Trent households. And the first thing they did was to help us identify our own balance points—the very thing we'll show you how to do next.

Finding Your Hard or Soft Tendencies

Later in the book, we'll be describing a number of specific ways you can balance the two sides of love and build strong, lasting relationships as a result.

But as when we're beginning a trip, we have to know where we're starting from. Otherwise, the best road map in the world won't help us.

That's why we've provided a means for you to discover your personal balance point—today. You'll see for yourself where you stand with regard to balancing the two sides of love.

In relating to others day to day, are you shifted to one extreme or the other? Are you camped out in the far reaches of a hardside life, easily issuing commands and criticism but not given to caring actions? Is it easy for you to be hard on problems but too easy to be hard on people as well?

In relating to others day to day, are you
shifted to one extreme or the other?

Or do you rarely move beyond an unhealthy softside, unwilling to confront someone or take the lead? Do you hesitate to act, even when you know you should be firm and others need you to be strong? Is your softness with people pushed so far that you're soft on the problems facing you and your family—even serious problems?

Perhaps most important, *do you know for a fact how those closest to you view you on an everyday basis?*

By taking the self-evaluation below, you can discover your personal balance point. You may not see a need for such self-examination, but others close to you probably do. So for them, if not for yourself, take the next five minutes and follow the simple instructions for filling in this instrument.

Discovering Your Personal Balance Point

Twenty pairs of words are listed below. To take the quiz, begin by thinking about the person closest to you (your spouse if you're married, or a close friend or parent if you're single). Then circle the number that best represents how you act toward that individual. Be sure to respond according to how you *currently and consistently* act toward that person, not according to how you *wish* you would or *occasionally* do act.

We also highly recommend that you have that same loved one fill in the instrument based on how *he or she* sees you. Then the two of you can discuss the results, noting especially any differences of perception that arise.

One man who has a strong personality scored himself squarely in the center of the softness scale the first time he took this quiz. However, when his wife evaluated him, he came out more like Attila the Hun than Mother Teresa. It took some time for his shock to wear off. But as they talked about their different perceptions of how he acted at home, it turned into one of the most enlightening and helpful discussions they'd ever had.

For additional insight, you may want to take the quiz again based on how you respond to each *child* in your home. If they're old enough, have them use it to rate you as well.

As we've developed this instrument, we've had entire families (with grade school or older children) sit around the dinner table and take it as part of a family night. Time and again, when there is freedom to discuss each other's scores—and the feelings and issues behind them—we've seen this experience begin to mend relationship fences and pull the family closer together.

Finally, be careful to look at this instrument as a window into people's lives, not as a weapon with which to attack. If you do find your loved ones shifted to an extreme, be careful not to belittle. It's usually better to let them discover where they are by taking the evaluation themselves than to point out their shortcomings for them.

Keep in mind that regardless of where you score today, you can move toward a healthy balance. We'll go into detail later on ten specific ways you can grow softer if you're currently too hard. And we'll also describe ten ways you can become more hardside if you presently display an unhealthy softness. There's plenty of room for all of us to grow when it comes to giving both sides of love.

Finding Your Personal Balance Point

Example:

Takes the lead   Follower

1   2   3   4   5   6   7

If you tend to take the lead in your relationship quickly and consistently, you would circle 1. If you tend to follow the other person's directions or wishes the majority of the time, you would circle 7. If you fall somewhere between the two extremes, you would circle whatever number best represents how you relate to your loved one.

A Hardside/Softside Evaluation

How do you tend to act in your relationship with

_____?
(Loved one's name)

1. Take the lead   Follow

   1   2   3   4   5   6   7

2. Forceful   Nondemanding

   1   2   3   4   5   6   7

3. Energetic   Reserved

   1   2   3   4   5   6   7

4. Strive to accomplish   Let others set
   personal goals   your goals

   1   2   3   4   5   6   7

5. Be self-controlled   Lack discipline

   1   2   3   4   5   6   7

6. Make quick decisions   Hesitate in making
                                        decisions

   1   2   3   4   5   6   7

---

7. Want to hear facts   Want to share feelings

   1   2   3   4   5   6   7

8. Be a motivator   Respond

   1   2   3   4   5   6   7

9. Be highly competitive   Be noncompetitive

   1   2   3   4   5   6   7

10. Be possessive   Share

   1   2   3   4   5   6   7

11. Be assertive   Be shy

   1   2   3   4   5   6   7

12. Express anger to others   Hold anger inside

   1   2   3   4   5   6   7

13. Resist correction   Be very teachable

   1   2   3   4   5   6   7

14. Share your opinions openly   Hide your true feelings

   1   2   3   4   5   6   7

15. Function well under pressure   Function poorly under pressure

   1   2   3   4   5   6   7

16. Lecture when the   Listen and comfort
    person is hurting

    1   2   3   4   5   6   7

17. Hold grudges   Forgive easily

    1   2   3   4   5   6   7

18. Set rigid standards   Set flexible standards

    1   2   3   4   5   6   7

19. Be hard on him (her)   Be soft on him (her)
    as a person

    1   2   3   4   5   6   7

20. Be hard on his (her)   Be soft on his (her)
    problems   problems

    1   2   3   4   5   6   7

Scoring the instrument:

The total of all the numbers circled = _____
Mark your total score with an "X" on the line
below.

Hardside		Intensity Index				Softside
20	40	60	80	100	120	140

Application project:

We encourage you to discuss how close or far apart you were in your scoring with your spouse or close friend.

Example:

Hardside   **Intensity Index**   Softside

X——————————————X————

| 20 | 40 | 60 | 80 | 100 | 120 | 140 |

Spouse (friend) viewed me   I viewed myself

Many people find themselves scoring in the 75 to 105 range. This often indicates an ability to give and take in expressing the two sides of love. Those scoring below 65 or above 115 typically express one side much more than the other. Regardless of where you scored, you'll find the material in later chapters very helpful in developing or maintaining the ability to express needed hardness or softness.

Remember that your score should be cross-checked by a loved one or close friend to see how that person views you. Time and again, we've seen people score themselves in the middle of the scale, while loved ones place them at one of the extremes.

If we're serious about building strong relationships, it's important to find our personal balance point. But that's just the first step in developing a wholehearted love. It's not enough simply to see where we are. We also need to know what brought us to that point and how to make changes if we're to balance the two sides of love.

In the next several chapters, we'll see that there's something else we need to discover that goes hand in hand with everything we've talked about so far. In fact, to be able to balance our love with others, we've got to understand what is perhaps the major factor that can push us toward either extreme.

We're referring to the particular personality strengths we all have as individuals. Some of us have a natural edge in being hardside with people when we need to, yet we struggle to show warmth and offer praise. For others, our natural style puts softness within easy reach, yet the hardness to face problems and take strong stands seems to slip through our fingers.

Clearly understanding our God-given temperaments brings to light common causes of family disharmony; provides practical handles for resolving long-standing friction in a home; dramatically increases our feelings of value for our loved ones and friends; and gives additional reasons to honor God. All this begins as we see how powerfully our natural strengths, pushed even slightly out of balance, affect our ability to give and receive the two sides of love.

3

Which Way Are
You Bent?

"I can't believe it. My relationship with my daughter is so different now. We've had the best six weeks we've had in years! Even my husband can't believe it. If only I'd known earlier what Jessica really needed."

It was a cold Tuesday night, and a group was gathering for its weekly Bible study. Talking to me (John) was an attractive, blonde woman in her early thirties who had raced over the minute she arrived.

"Six weeks ago," she said, "I heard your presentation in another group about the need to give the two sides of love. I took the test you gave, and I could see that I'm good at being hard on problems.

But that day I also saw how I was being too hard on people—especially my daughter.

"Jessica is eleven, and she turned out to have very different natural strengths from mine. When I saw that, I realized that all her life, I'd been putting pressure on her to go faster and do more, and she's gone slower and done less than I wanted. I finally understood how different she is from me. She has a deep need to do things right and finish one project before going on to the next, but until now, it's never been something I valued.

"You can ask my husband," she said, putting her arm around the man who had just walked up. "He used to be the referee in our home, keeping Jessica and me from each other's throats. But these past six weeks, I've stopped using a timer to hurry her up with her homework or telling her to 'Just write anything' on a thank-you note so we can mail it out. I've started praising her for being so precise instead of criticizing her for it.

"I finally feel like I understand her, and it's changed our whole relationship," she continued, beaming. "In fact, it's motivated me to go from a too-hardside person to softer than I've ever been!"

What made such a major difference in this woman's relationship with her daughter? She already knew (and the test she took confirmed) that she was extremely hardside by nature. But by taking the next step and discovering her basic personality strengths, she learned several things that helped bring her love into balance and caused positive changes in her daughter's life. And the truths she learned can make a real difference in your relationships as well.

- *You'll discover a major reason people are pushed out of balance either hardside or softside, and how to correct the problem.*

Children seem to come fully equipped with a God-given personality bent, and even as adults, we tend to express our bent clearly. For example, Proverbs 22:6 is a familiar verse that reads, "Train a child in the way he should go, and when he is old he will not turn from it."

In the original language of the Old Testament, that verse actually reads, "Train up a child *according to his bent . . ."* So pronounced are these natural bents that a man we highly respect, Dr. Ross Campbell, feels you can even spot them in a newborn![1]

In just a few pages, we'll show how you can discover your own personality strengths. We've provided a one-page test that can help you recognize and value another person's strengths, as well as your own, in a way you may never have before. In sharing this test with thousands of singles and couples across the country, we've seen the resulting insight bring many couples and families closer together instantly.

In addition to discovering your natural strengths, you'll see how, when taken to extremes, they can push you out of balance either hardside or softside. Of the four natural bents people display, two tend to push us out of balance toward the hard side. People with these bents tend to be hard on problems. Unfortunately, they can be very hard on people as well.

The other two types of people lean toward the soft side in relationships. Their natural strength is being supportive. But they're often much too soft on problems that demand a hardside response.

By taking the simple self-survey we've provided, you'll be able to see what your own and other people's natural strengths are. Then, aided by the chapters that follow, you'll be able to tell which way you have a natural tendency to drift. But those are only two benefits you'll gain by taking this survey. There are more.

Many family conflicts are caused by viewing another person's natural strengths as weaknesses.

- *Starting with the very next chapter, you'll be able to sense immediately what's at the heart of many family conflicts—and see how to solve them.*

It's incredible how many family conflicts are caused by viewing another person's natural strengths as weaknesses. A clear view of what naturally motivates another person can open the door to greater compassion, patience, compromise and caring. What's more, you'll see how people's natural personality strengths, just slightly out of balance, can become their biggest weaknesses and most irritating behaviors. Knowing that can be very helpful, particularly when there's stress or tension around the house.

Different temperaments handle tension in different ways. For example, the two natural bents that lean toward being hardside often become more controlling of people and the situation. If that fails, they're not above picking up their marbles and moving away from the problem altogether. However, the two bents that lean toward the soft side often either give in (or up) too quickly or become very verbal and emotional to try to get their way.

- *You'll gain a handle on dealing with your own weaknesses.*

Can you think of a past or present problem area in your life? If we asked you to write your three greatest weaknesses on a 3 X 5 card, could you do it? Many of us would just be getting warmed up if we listed only three! In fact, we'd start looking for legal pads to write them all!

Most people, particularly most Christians, are experts in understanding their weaknesses. But without realizing it, by focusing on their weaknesses, they're effectively blocking their ability to deal with those very problem areas. That's because *there is no way to overcome a weakness without first knowing our strengths*. Why?

Almost without exception, our weaknesses are simply a reflection of our strengths being pushed to an extreme. For example, a softside bent often includes the ability to listen closely and carefully to others. But pushed to an extreme, this positive trait can become a weakness. At times, our focus on listening can keep us from asking the hard questions we should. We can also listen so much to others' problems that we become overburdened or never take the time to verbalize our own hurts and concerns.

Another person may possess the natural hardside bent of being a critical thinker. Held in balance, that talent can make him great at dissecting things or projects. But push that strength out of balance and the ability to take issues apart can be used to take people apart as well.

By using the personal evaluation form at the end of this chapter, you'll see your strengths more clearly or in a different light. In fact, we've seen many people, after taking this test, learn for the first time to value the way God uniquely created them.

• *You'll discover a major key to Christlikeness.*

Discovering more about these natural bents can also help us see the love of Christ in a clearer, deeper way. How?

For one thing, the way Jesus dealt with others demonstrated that He had the strengths of all four basic personalities held in balance. Seeing those bents in perfection in His person can both challenge us and draw us closer to Him than ever before.

Using Our Strengths to Balance Love

We know a number of good personality tests are available today. In all, we've examined more than thirty different instruments that can give you a helpful reading of your basic temperament.

For our purposes here, however, we're looking at personality types through a much different lens. That's why we came up with our own instrument to help you see clearly how your strengths specifically affect your ability to give both sides of love to your family and friends.

If, after taking our short survey, you want a more in-depth analysis of your personality, one instrument we recommend highly is the "Pro Scan" PDP survey. Dr. Mike Williamson, a committed Christian and close friend of Dr. James Dobson, helped create this extremely reliable test that provides a detailed, ten-page analysis. While it is geared primarily toward helping people identify their personality strengths and stresses in the workplace, it can also be adapted to the home situation. (For more information about how to obtain this and other personality surveys, see the Notes section at the back of the book.[2])

Almost without exception, our weaknesses
are a reflection of our strengths being
pushed to an extreme.

In creating our survey, we tried to be sensitive to two important concerns. First, we feel strongly that behavior cannot always be neatly categorized and labeled. Personality types don't all fit into four distinct boxes. That's why we emphasize that each person is really a blend of all four natural bents. In fact, even though most people will have one or perhaps two primary personality bents, each of us needs to be able to tap into all four to build strong relationships.

People usually see themselves in one category, with a second bent as present but less dominant. Our goal, however, isn't to restrict behavior by labeling it. Rather, we hope the labels illustrate where we are today so that we can more easily use the strengths of all the bents tomorrow in providing others with both sides of love.

Second, we wanted to capture these natural bents in a way that would be easily understood and remembered. That's why we chose to picture them by using animals.

It was Corrie ten Boom who inspired us never to teach without using objects. Again, as a way of staying away from restrictive labels, we like using animal names to breathe life into the different bents. If you dislike being pictured in a fun-loving way as one of God's furry creatures, feel free to change the descriptive titles to something with which you're more comfortable.

With all that in mind, we invite you to take the Personal Strengths Survey. In doing so, you'll see firsthand what your natural strengths are. What's more, you'll begin to see how you can blend your natural strengths with those of others in your home.

How to Take the Personal Strengths Survey

We've tried to make taking this survey as simple as possible, which isn't true of all tests. For example, one popular personality test has more than three hundred questions, asking things like "Do you smell things that other people don't?" and "When you watch television, do the people talk back to you?"

In the Personal Strengths Survey, all we ask is that you circle a few simple words describing yourself. Then, with that information, we'll show you specifically what your unique strengths are and why they make you such a valuable person in all your relationships.

To complete the instrument, just read through the four boxes on pages 48–49 (the L, B, O and G boxes), and *circle* each *word or phrase that seems to describe a consistent character trait of yours.* Next, add up the number of words and phrases you circled in each box. Then there's only one more step: you *double your score* to come up with a total in each box. What could be easier?

If that's all the instruction you need, go ahead and take the survey. But if you're the type of person who thinks these things should be more complicated, here are some additional details.

As you'll notice, each box has fourteen words or word groups (like "Takes charge," "determined" and "firm") and one phrase (like "Let's do it now!").

In the first box (with an *L* above it), you might read each word or phrase and decide to circle only one word as representing a fairly consistent character trait of yours. On the other hand, you might decide that all fourteen words and even the phrase apply to you. In that case, you would end up with all fifteen choices circled.

Go through each box, circling as many words and phrases as describe who you are consistently. Then double the number of words you circled to come up with a total score for each.

Remember that if you don't circle at least one word or phrase in one of the four boxes, you probably don't have a personality! (And that's a problem beyond the scope of this book!)

Finally, take the total scores from all the boxes and transfer them to the graph below the survey. The last thing left is something that most of us enjoy doing: connect the dots!

As you take this short self-survey, keep two things in mind. First, circle your responses based on how you relate to the people in your family— the most important people in your life. However, you may also want to make a copy of this inventory and take it again based on how you respond to people at work. Why?

Many people tend to shift their actions and atti-

tudes between home and work. We've seen many men, for example, who are extremely hardside at work but who go home and are out of balance softside. You may discover that having to be one way at home and another at work is the source of much of your personal stress.

Second, be sure to circle responses based on who you actually are and how you act toward others right now—not on how you *wish* you were or always *wanted* to be. Some surveys and testing instruments include elaborate "lie" scales to make a person be honest in taking a test. We haven't chosen to do that with ours.

Can you make yourself look "better" than you really are on this survey? Certainly. Should you? Not if you want an honest evaluation of who you are and how you relate to others. That's one reason we ask people to have a loved one or close friend fill out the survey based on how *they* see them: it's a way of getting a more-objective analysis.

The Personal Strengths Survey

Once again, in each box, circle every word or phrase that describes a consistent character trait of yours. Total the number circled in each box, then double your score. Next, take the total score from each box and put it on the graph. Take a few minutes now to complete the survey and fill in the graph before continuing.

* * *

After you've taken the instrument and transferred your scores to the chart, what does it all mean?

The four letters at the top of each section stand for the four basic personality types we'll describe in more detail in the chapters that follow. Each holds a key to whether we tend to be hard or soft in relationships. As you'll see, everyone is a combination of all four of these types. But for now, let's take a quick overview of the four animals.

Scoring high on the L line are those we call *lions*. Lions are take-charge leaders. They're usually the bosses at work, or at least they think they are! They're decisive, bottom-line folks who are doers, not watchers or listeners. They love to solve problems. Unfortunately, however, if they don't learn to use both sides of love, their natural hardside bent can cause problems with others.

Scoring high on the B line are those we call *beavers*. Beavers have a strong need to do things "right" and "by the book." In fact, they're the kind of people who actually read instruction manuals! They like maps, charts and organization. And they're great at providing quality control for a home or office.

Because rules, consistency and high standards are so important to beavers, they often communicate the hard side of love to others just like the lion. Beavers have deep feelings for those they love. But learning to balance the two sides of love usually involves adding the ability to communicate that softness and warmth in a way that's felt and clearly understood by others.

Scoring high on the O line are the *otters*. Otters are excitable, fun-seeking, cheerleader types who love to yak, yak, yak. They're great at motivating others and need to be in an environment where they get to talk and have a vote on major decisions.

Otters' outgoing nature makes them great networkers—they usually know people who know people who know people. The only problem is, they usually don't know everyone's name! They can be very soft and encouraging with others (unless under pressure, when they tend to use their verbal skills to attack). But because of their strong desire to be liked, they can often fail to be hard on problems and cause further problems as a result.

Scoring high on the G line are the *golden retrievers*. These people are just like their counterparts in nature. If you could pick one word to describe them, it would be *loyalty*. They're so loyal, in fact, that they can absorb *the* most emotional pain and punishment in relationships—and still stay committed. They're great listeners, empathizers and warm encouragers—all strong softside skills. But they tend to be such pleasers that they can have great difficulty in adding the hard side of love when it's needed.

With all these animals running around in families, churches and offices, life can be like a zoo! So how can we go about taming our own version of

L Takes charge   Bold
Determined   Purposeful
Assertive   Decision maker
Firm   Leader   "Let's do
Enterprising   Goal driven   it now!"
Competitive   Self-reliant
Enjoys challenges   Adventurous

Double the number circled _____

B Deliberate   Discerning
Controlled   Detailed
Reserved   Analytical   "How was
Predictable   Inquisitive   it done in
Practical   Precise   the past?"
Orderly   Persistent
Factual   Scheduled

Double the number circled _____

O Takes risks   Fun-loving
Visionary   Likes variety
Motivator   Enjoys change   "Trust me!
Energetic   Creative   It'll work
Very verbal   Group oriented   out!"
Promoter   Mixes easily
Avoids details   Optimistic

Double the number circled _____

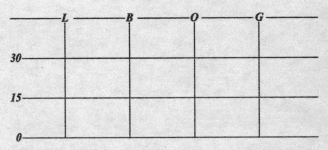

G	Loyal	Adaptable	
	Nondemanding	Sympathetic	"Let's keep
	Even keel	Thoughtful	things the
	Avoids conflict	Nurturing	way they
	Enjoys routine	Patient	are."
	Dislikes change	Tolerant	
	Deep relationships	Good listener	

Double the number circled _____

Personal Strengths Survey Chart

	L	B	O	G
30				
15				
0				

"The Wild Kingdom"? As you'll see beginning in the next chapter, the answer comes through learning how each of these personalities can give the two sides of love, as well as what can block them from doing so.

Let's look first at the two animals that display most naturally love's hard side, lions and beavers, and how they tend to respond in family and work relationships. After that, we'll turn our focus toward the two animals that tend to reflect love's soft side, otters and golden retrievers. Then we'll consider ten specific ways hardside people can learn to add softness to their lives, followed by ten specific ways softside people can add the loving hardness they need.

It all begins as we take a look at those people who often reflect a "king of the jungle" attitude in business and personal relationships—our lion friends.

4

Discovering the Strengths of a Lion

Lions possess a number of admirable hardside strengths. They're decisive, purposeful and great at conquering nearly any challenge. As with the other personalities, however, if their strengths get pushed out of balance, those traits can become their greatest weaknesses.

We recently heard the life-changing story of an eight-year-old boy whose father had scored off the chart on the lion scale. This man was the service manager for his company, but he knew in his heart that one day he'd be the owner. His drive to accomplish things at work kept him away from the house most of every day, willing to hand out only emotional leftovers to his wife and children.

On a rare Saturday morning off, this man was seated in his favorite chair, reading his paper, when his son walked up.

For several moments, this young boy stood right next to his father without saying a word. His hardside dad tried his best to ignore him, putting on his sternest face. Finally, however, when he realized his son wasn't going to go away, he put down his paper and said roughly, "Now what do you want?"

His son smiled and held out a handful of crumpled dollar bills and assorted change. "Here, Daddy," he said, dropping them into his father's outstretched palm.

"What's this for?" the father asked.

"This is all I have in my piggy bank. It's eight dollars and fifty-four cents. Daddy, it's all yours if you'll just stay home and play with me today."

This lion father had spent all his days putting work ahead of his family. And when he wasn't working, he was resting to work. He didn't take time to play with his son because he didn't feel he was "accomplishing" anything by playing. But his son finally hit him right in his heart when he realized an eight-year-old was willing to give everything he had for some of Dad's time.

Traits of the Typical Lion

Not all lions are as hard as this man, of course. From a very early age, however, seven characteristics stand out in the typical lion's behavior. What's more, they tend to carry right into marriage and the workplace.

These strengths help lions to be naturally hard on problems. But the major challenge lions face is to add enough softness to their natural style to keep from being too hard on people in the process. What are these common characteristics of a lion?

1. Lions are born leaders.

Do you ever get the feeling that your son or daughter is letting you live at home? If so, you're probably the parent of a lion. From a young age, lions like to be in charge. As they grow up, they naturally gravitate to leadership positions in school, at work and at church. They definitely feel more comfortable if they're the ones calling the shots. As one lion friend told us, "Ever since grade school, I've never met a group I couldn't lead!"

Lions tend to be self-motivated and don't need a great deal to keep them going. In fact, like Peter and Paul in the Scriptures, they simply need to be pointed the right way! They're already headed in a specific direction, usually their own, and expecting others to follow.

Lions are so leadership oriented that they often resist being controlled by anyone else. As children, their parents often think about pasting their pictures on the cover of Dr. Dobson's book *The Strong-Willed Child*. And while this characteristic can help them be strong and independent in later life, it's crucial they learn that the best leaders know how to follow as well. If nothing else, they need to remind themselves that everyone has a boss, even if your only boss is God.

Over the years, we've met many Christian leaders. Can you guess whom you often find at the top of ministries and churches? Lions. They've taken their natural hardside strength of leadership and used it to charge ahead with a vision or to inspire leadership in others. But leadership isn't their only desire or strength.

Lions feel very strongly that life is a series of problems they need to solve or challenges they need to meet.

---

2. Lions like to accomplish things with immediate results.

Some parents have told us that their lion children began issuing orders the moment they came out of the womb, and that may not be far off.[1] But lions like to take charge and be in control for a specific reason: *they feel very strongly that life is a series of problems they need to solve or challenges they need to meet.*

This powerful desire to accomplish something often means they can do the seemingly impossible. In fact, the easiest way to motivate lions is to tell them a job can't be done, then stand back and watch them accomplish it.

What does this strength mean when applied in a home setting? For one thing, most lions desperately need to learn that relaxation is not a crime. It's terribly hard for them to take it easy around the house. They usually have a demanding hobby or a challenging project they're working on. And if a project isn't at hand, they can choose their spouses or children as "projects" and begin trying to change or "motivate" them.

One young woman told her father, "Dad, every time you talk to me, I feel as if you're trying to change me or force me into becoming something I'm not. When are we ever going to talk without you giving me instructions the whole time?"

For most lions, even vacations can be something to attack! Take a vacation to the mountains, and instead of going to one or two of the sites, they want to hike every trail. Head for the beach, and they'll do anything except lie out in the sun. Why? Because lying in the sun doesn't *accomplish* anything.

This inner drive to accomplish tasks can help lions achieve great things. When pushed to an extreme, however, this strength can lead to elevating *projects* far ahead of *people* and laying the foundation for hardside workaholism.

3. A lion's time frame is *now!*

For the average lion, taking the lead in conquering projects or problems isn't enough. They have to be conquered *now*.

If you work for a boss who's a lion, she's capable of walking over to your desk, handing you a project, and saying, "I want you to do this now."

"But Boss," you might say, "you just gave me a project to work on."

"I know," would come the reply, "but that was twenty minutes ago. I want you to work on this *now!*"

Take this characteristic into a home setting, and dinner needs to be ready *now*. My diapers need to be changed *now*. Give me the remote control or change the channel *now*. You need to stop crying, take my advice, and grow up *now*.

What's communicated as people see lions' natural *now* orientation? Often it's hardside intensity. It's easy for lions to become so intense just working on a project (or simply thinking about the next important project) that they look mad to others, even if they aren't.

The average lion can radiate so much intensity that, as you'll see, golden retrievers and otters will learn to shy away from approaching or asking questions. They'll even avoid initiating important conversations because of the hardside nonverbal signals a lion can send out.

Sometimes lions will use this nonverbal intensity level as a shield from "stupid" questions or interruptions. However, if they're not careful, using their natural intensity to gain emotional "space" will quickly leave them isolated at best and resented at worst.

Speaking of resentment, we know of one lion on a church board who made a *now* decision that had major effects on a number of people far into the future. It all started with one of the most helpful times the church staff had ever experienced, but it wasn't to end that way. Even the word *disastrous* doesn't convey what happened.

For the first time ever, the senior pastor, all five of his associates and all their wives had gone to a neighboring city for a weekend together. With months to prepare for the trip, the pulpit and all the various class and counseling responsibilities had been farmed out to capable hands. At long last, an overdue opportunity to draw closer together as friends and ministry partners had taken shape— and they even had a weekend off!

Even the drive to the hotel helped bond these men and women whose ministries had become like six individual islands over the years. One car had a flat tire, requiring everyone to pitch in and get them back on the road. Another car (with the senior pastor's wife) set the record for most breaks in a fifty-mile trip by stopping at nine antique shops along the way.

When they all finally arrived, there was a scrumptious dinner awaiting them and a meaningful worship time that night in one of the rooms.

The time together went from being good to great the next morning. Following breakfast, they all gathered for an emotional meeting in which husbands and wives shared their pent-up feelings and frustrations. Apologies were offered and accepted, hugs asked for and given. The genuine spirit of love and restoration swept aside any cobwebs of misunderstanding, making everyone feel more like a team than ever before.

By the time each couple arrived home late Sunday evening, they were excited and enthusiastic about their various ministries. But that was soon to change.

Little did the pastors know that while they were gone, a purebred lion had been on the loose. In fact, the chairman of their elder board redefined the breed.

This man had been to a management effectiveness seminar for his business on the very Friday the pastors left for their retreat. Impressed with what he heard, in his mind's eye he saw what he thought were profound applications for both his business and the church. That's why, without hesitation or consultation, he had made up his mind what needed to be done.

While the pastors were out of town, he called in all the maintenance people, as well as several "starving student" movers. Then he set out to make the church more "effective" and "efficient," beginning with redesigning the church office.

What that meant in practical terms was that when the six pastors walked in on Monday morning, a surprise was waiting for them. When they put their keys in their doors and opened their offices, it was as if they had entered—The Twilight Zone.

The keys fit, and they were standing in front of the right doors, but they were no longer looking at their own offices. They shook their heads in disbelief as they stared at a different pastor's things all set up in what used to be their offices! Not only had every office been changed, but several secretarial relationships were also switched, splitting up some pastors and their secretaries who had worked together for five and six years.

The chairman of their elder board never thought of asking for a meeting to discuss the changes he wanted to make. It wasn't that he wasn't a good man. It was just that he saw what he thought was a problem, discovered a solution at his morning seminar, and the movers were at work that afternoon!

Lions will do well to make a consistent priority check on how much involvement they give their loved ones in decisions that affect them; it's an important part of softside love. They'll also do well to make sure their natural *now* tendency doesn't sacrifice a healthy future in their relationships.

4. Lions are decisive.

Tied in with their need to lead, control, accomplish and do things now, lions generally make decisions quickly—with or without the facts, and often without asking anyone for advice.

In the home, it's often great to have someone around who isn't afraid to make decisions, even difficult ones. But in some cases, that natural tendency toward being decisive can be pushed far out of balance.

We know of one wife who experienced something even worse than what happened to that church staff. Carol and her husband, Mark, had finally saved up enough money to make a down payment on their first house. They had picked out a small starter home they both liked, and the day came when they were to meet at the title company office to put down their deposit and sign the papers.

Carol was beside herself with excitement as she waited for the morning to drag by until their afternoon appointment. She was just starting to gather her things to meet Mark at the title company when she heard a horn beeping outside. Looking out the window, she didn't recognize the shiny, new truck that sat in the driveway. But as she stepped outside, she saw Mark behind the wheel.

"Where did you get that?" Carol asked in shock as she walked up to her grinning husband.

"Carol," he said almost flippantly, "I know we were going to use all that money for that house, but you'll never guess what kind of deal I got on this truck!"

That morning, Carol's lion husband had gone to the bank to withdraw their money and take it to the title company. But he had stopped at the local car dealership "just to look" on the way home. In a few minutes' time (and with a little pressure from a hungry salesman), he had made a decision to buy the truck instead of the house. And, it goes without saying, he made the decision without bothering to consult his wife.

When she pleaded with him to take the truck back, he told her, "Listen, I made my decision. It's not up for a vote, and that's final. Besides, I wasn't all that hot on that house anyway, and you know I really needed a new truck for work."

Mark had his new truck that didn't bear a scratch or dent on it. But little did he know that as he drove off to work, he had just smashed his wife's heart and nearly totaled out his marriage by not involving her in a major decision.

When the pressure is on, one of the great hardside strengths of lions is that they can act quickly and decisively. We need such leaders; we have far too few of them in our churches and homes today. We sometimes even need people who can step out in faith without first gathering every possible fact. But leadership is more than being strong and forceful. It doesn't take an advanced degree in insensitivity to be considered a strong leader.

We encourage lions to read the final chapter in this book to see how the Lion of Judah balanced His purposeful decisiveness with compassionate, softside understanding.

5. Lions want *Readers Digest*-length communication.

Perhaps it's their decisive attitude that makes most lions gag at small talk. One woman with a great deal of lion in her told us how frustrated she was with her golden retriever husband.

"When I ask him, 'How's your day been?' all I want is a one-page version of what happened. But every time I ask, I get the whole book of *War and Peace!*"

That same frustration is felt by many lion men.

Often a wife will try to talk with her lion husband about something less "important" than nuclear disarmament or solving the federal budget deficit and be cut off in midsentence.

She may try saying something about one of the kid's days or her own and hear something like, "Honey, what are we trying to *solve* here?" Or if her spouse is really insensitive to the impact of his words, she may even hear something like, "Dear, I don't mind talking with you, but next time, let's talk about something important!"

For lions, meaningful communication usually equals short sentences, sticking to the point, and getting on to something more important than talking—namely, charging ahead and "doing" something rather than discussing it. Their natural desire for efficient conversation must be balanced with the time needed to generate softsided, relational communication. That means listening closely and with acceptance, not jumping in with a hardside lecture or solution.

6. Lions often feel challenged by questions.

Several years ago, a man and his wife went to an auction with some friends. Several hundred people were standing outside, ready to jam into the building holding the auction. The woman had a special need for a kitchen table and chairs, and she was looking forward to getting a great deal on an oak or maple set.

The doors finally opened, and in the rush of people going into the pavilion, the woman and their friends got separated from her husband. After trying hard to find him, at last they decided to sit down and watch some of the bidding.

Within a short time, the crowd began bidding on furniture, and one of the first items to come up was a dilapidated, green kitchen table and chair set. With its pea-green vinyl and rust-pitted legs, it had obviously seen its best days years ago. But strangely, the price kept going up and up as two men the woman couldn't see got into a bidding war over this nearly worthless dinette set.

When the final bid was made and the gavel slammed down, the woman leaned over and said to her friends, "I can't believe anybody would pay that much for that piece of junk!"

That's when the man who had just bought the green monstrosity stood up, and—you guessed it—it was the woman's husband!

"Henry," she said when they finally caught up with him, "that's the ugliest table and chairs I've ever seen! Why in the world did you buy that without talking to me? I wanted a *wooden* table, not a vinyl one. What were you thinking?"

The man instantly grew defensive. The only answer he gave her was, "You needed a table and chairs, I bought them, and that settles it!"

Asking a question of an out-of-balance lion is often interpreted as a personal challenge, not a reasonable request for information. Unfortunately, many lions marry people whom God has given a natural bent toward question asking—our golden retriever and beaver friends.

Denying those folks the right to ask questions is a great way to hardside them—to close their spirits and slam the door on meaningful relationship.[2] Lions need to slow down long enough to look at all sides of an issue. They also need to realize that developing a loving home is more important than simply demanding everyone's loyalty. Finally, they should make sure they don't interpret the deep need of a beaver or golden retriever for clarification as a challenge to their authority.

7. Lions are not afraid of pressure or confrontation.

As you may have sensed by now, in their quest for challenge and accomplishments, quick decisions and instant communication, lions can put a great deal of pressure on themselves and others. And while some people (like beavers and golden retrievers) are very uncomfortable with feeling pressured, lions thrive on tension.

A lion friend who owns a fairly large company confessed to us, "I get bored when things are going too smoothly around the office. In fact, my staff has often accused me of breaking things just so I can fix them!"

Put this tendency to pressure people alongside their natural lack of fear of confrontation, and *unless they're careful, lions can hardside and hurt other people's feelings without even realizing it.*

We once counseled a couple in which the man, a strong lion, was used to roaring at those at work and at home and always getting his way. He was extremely wealthy and owned his own company, so no one he employed was willing to question his pressure tactics. With three golden retrievers at home (his wife and two young children), no one there was willing to stand up to him, either.

In our first session together, we quickly saw by the way he treated his wife that he was an out-of-balance lion. He made a tremendous amount of money, but he kept her on a budget that wouldn't even get her through the grocery store checkout. And instead of being an encouragement to her or the kids, he came close to terrorizing them with his harsh language and attitudes.

Deep down, this man did love his family, but he didn't know how to show it. And it's no wonder. He came from a home where his own father used fear and intimidation every day, and he was simply passing down to his family the hurt he had felt as a child.

After listening for almost an hour to the story of his background and to his wife's concerns, I (John) made the comment that the primary way he communicated was by intimidating people.

Instantly he stood up, grabbed the edge of the table, and leaned over toward me. "My goal isn't to intimidate anybody!" he shouted, staring at me with venom in his eyes. "What do you know, anyway? You're just a *kid*."

I do have a youthful appearance, and that wasn't the first time I'd heard that comment. As a trained counselor, I knew how important it was to remain calm and understanding over such remarks. But something happened in that counseling office that has never happened before or since.

In the months that have passed, I've searched my heart to see if what I did was wrong. But in this case, I still feel the Lord was giving me the strength of a lion to deal with what was happening before me.

Without thinking, I stood up, grabbed the edge of the table in front of me, and leaned over toward *him*. "Your goal *is* to intimidate people," I said firmly. "And the problem is that it's worked for you. You've got everyone so afraid of you that they won't call you out or tell you you're wrong."

"Is that right?" he said, his voice dripping with sarcasm.

"That's right," I said even more firmly, looking at him eye to eye. "Now get this straight. You're killing your family with your words and your anger. Intimidation may have worked for you for a long time and kept you from being confronted, but it's not going to work in here."

"You think you can talk to me like that!" he roared, clenching his fists, standing up, and shifting his weight as if to draw back and take a swing.

I had fought a good deal in my non-Christian background, and I could tell that push had come to shove. He wasn't just mad; he was livid. I dropped my hands from the table, getting ready for the fight I knew was coming. At that moment, I fully believed we were going to get into a free-for-all right there in the counseling room, and I was ready.

Gary's eyes widened and his jaw dropped as he watched us.

For what seemed like hours (but was actually only a few seconds), there was absolute silence in the room. We held each others' stares, refusing to look away and knowing what one move toward the other would mean. You could have cut the tension with a chain saw, as this man's wife and Gary sat transfixed at the table, not knowing if we were going to start throwing punches.

Finally, the man chuckled out loud, unclenched his fists, and sat down. "John," he said with a smile and a calm voice, "nobody has talked to me like that in years!

"You're right, you know," he continued, his voice softer than it had been all morning. "I've always been a bully. I probably don't know how to relate to someone other than by getting angry."

The tension had begun to ease in the room, and Gary and the man's wife were starting to breathe again, when suddenly the man sat forward, pointed his finger at her, and with his most-threatening voice said, "Why can't you learn to stand up to me like he does? Then we wouldn't be in this mess!"

All was not lost, however. That morning, they made a major breakthrough in their relationship. This man was very comfortable with pressure, and even with major confrontation. But he had finally learned that his natural hardside power could easily cross the line into intimidation, even when that wasn't his intent.

In cases like this, lions can be so strong that they

win every verbal battle but end up losing the war and the prize of their family's hearts.

To review, we've seen that seven characteristics commonly surface in lions' lives. Namely:

1. Lions are born leaders.
2. Lions like to accomplish things with immediate results.
3. Lions' time frame is now!
4. Lions are decisive.
5. Lions want *Reader's Digest*-length communication.
6. Lions often feel threatened by questions.
7. Lions are not afraid of pressure or confrontation.

Lions can be so strong that they win every verbal battle but end up losing the war for their family's hearts.

Lions' #1 Relational Challenge

One time we (John and Cindy) took our daughter Kari to the local zoo. To get an overview of what animals they had, we rode a tram that goes past all the exhibits. Not surprisingly, the largest crowd was assembled at the lion compound.

People are fascinated with lions of both the animal and human kind. The problem is that once lions roar, others can easily become afraid of them as well. Many lions are kept at an emotional arm's length because they seem distant, angry, unapproachable or all three.

In the midst of a war, we need field generals who can inspire and lead. With life and death in the balance, results and decisive action—even strutting and shouting at times—can become more important than sensitive relationships.

Unfortunately, some out-of-balance lions forget that their homes should normally be places of peace, and a few actually seem to declare war on their families. They demand unquestioned allegiance and expect others to follow their orders immediately. What's more, they view questions as a sign of disloyalty and, in some cases, as grounds for desertion. They desire "bottom line" communication without realizing that the real bottom line in a home is whether the other person goes away feeling loved and understood.

We're here to say that it's possible to become a sensitive lion without sacrificing the natural strengths God has built into a person. In fact, we've seen firsthand examples of it over and over. And we've seen that while people will follow any effective leader to a point, they'll go to the wall for a strong leader who loves them.

Every home, office and church needs the hardside strengths of a lion. But the Lion of Judah led in such a way that His hardside strengths didn't sacrifice His softside skill of giving unconditional love and acceptance to others (more about that later).

The challenge for lions is not to pull out all their

claws. Instead, it's to balance their lion strengths with the love of the Lamb of God. Then they can see great things happen in their relationships.

We've looked at the first personality bent that leans toward being hardside. The second is that of our beaver friends, who like to "live by the book." Their strengths are many, but they, too, need to learn how they can give and receive the two sides of love.

5

Discovering the Strengths of a Beaver

As we skidded our bicycles to a stop in front of our house, my twin brother and I (John) looked up and saw the same thing. There it was—one pitiless eye staring right at us. Without a word being spoken, we both knew we were in major trouble—again.

As a child, I hated living on the street corner. It wasn't that our home wasn't nice. But owning the corner house meant the street light was planted right in our yard.

"Be home before the street light comes on!" was the ironclad law. No "fudge factor" was allowed. My grandfather would have scored at the top of the charts in the hardsided beaver category, and he lived life by the rules. All he had to do was look out the window and see if we'd made it home in time. And once again, we hadn't.

I know that for today's parents, the topic of spanking is often controversial. But when I grew up, there wasn't even a mild discussion. My grandfather had come to help my mother raise three rambunctious boys in a single-parent home, and he believed firmly in spanking. And in his rule book, being late for dinner was a two-swat offense.

My grandfather shared a number of characteristics with other beavers. They tend to be reserved in their relationships, playing their emotional cards close to the vest. They're detailed, cautious, and like to look at all sides of an issue.

As I grew up, I saw his attention to rules and emotional reserve as hardside weaknesses, not personal strengths. I often interpreted his tendency to be quiet and thoughtful as being cold and distant. But at least you were always sure of where you stood with him. You could depend on him to be predictable in his actions, emotions and attitude.

That's why, as I shuffled down the hallway to Grandfather's room, I knew exactly what was going to happen: two swats on the bottom with his old-style razor strap. Little did I know that one of the greatest times of blessing in my life lay ahead as well.

1. Beavers keep a close watch on their emotions.

After my spanking, my mother told me to go back down the hall and call my grandfather for dinner. While I didn't feel much like talking to him at the time, I didn't want to risk another spanking, either. So off I went to his room.

Many children grow up calling their grandfather "Gramps," "Grandpa," "Papa" or some other affectionate nickname. Not us. There were rules of respect to be observed in our home, and any time we addressed him, we were to call him "Grandfather" or "Sir."

What's more, it was a two-swat offense to enter his room without first knocking politely at the door and waiting outside until he gave us permission to enter.

I was about to knock when I noticed his door was already slightly ajar. That's why I broke the cardinal rule and gently pushed it open to look inside.

What I saw shocked me. My grandfather, a man who rarely showed any emotion, was sitting on the end of his bed, crying. I stood at the door in confusion, not knowing what to say. Suddenly, he looked up and saw me, and I froze where I was. I had no idea what was coming when he spoke to me.

"Come here, John," he said, his voice full of emotion. I walked over, fully expecting to be disciplined for not knocking. But instead of swatting me, he reached out and took me in his arms.

Grandfather hugged me closely, and in tears he told me how much he loved each of us boys and how deeply it hurt him to have to spank us. I had no idea why he always stayed in his room for a few minutes after disciplining us. Now I knew. He spent the time alone; sometimes crying, always praying that we would grow up to be the men God wanted us to be.

"John," he told me, seating me on the bed next to him and putting his big arms around me, "I want more than anything in life for each of you to become godly young men. I've done all I could to help you know what's right, and to encourage you to live your life by God's rules.

"I won't always be here to remind you. Besides, you're a young man now. I hope you know how much I love you, how proud I am of you, and how much I pray for each of you boys. I know you'll always be the man God wants you to be throughout your life."

I can't explain it, but when I left his room that night, I was a different person. As I look back today, that evening provided me with a meaningful rite of passage from childhood to young adulthood. For years afterward, recalling that clear picture of my grandfather's love helped to shape my attitudes and actions.

A few months later, in that same room, Grandfather died instantly and unexpectedly. I thank God that I didn't make it home that night before the street light turned on. I know now that the Lord allowed me to experience a time of blessing with the most important man in my early life.

Like others high on the beaver scale, my grandfather was reserved, cautious and controlled when it came to displaying emotions and affection. He was also sparing with his praise. But that night, I felt as if the veil had lifted. I got to see the soft side of his heart in a way I never had before. He let down his structured responses and tightly held feelings in a spontaneous act of emotion, and it made a major impact on my life.

It's not that beavers have a difficult time loving others. Their commitment to those they love can be just as strong as that of our loyal golden retriever friends. However, beavers often have difficulty communicating that softside warmth to others.

If you're a beaver and you find yourself standing back in relationships, you'll want to read chapters 10 and 11 on developing a healthy softness. But for now, let's look at several other characteristics that describe this important member of the family zoo.

2. Beavers actually read instruction books.

Besides keeping a close watch on their emotions, people who score high on the beaver scale tend to have something else in common. They're the ones who carefully read instruction manuals instead of throwing them away. Not all animals in the family zoo have this same strong desire to do things "by the book," however—especially otters.

Cindy and I (John) had been talking about putting up a swing set in the backyard for our daughter. It was early on a Saturday morning, and as Kari stumbled into the kitchen for her pancakes, I made a typical, overly optimistic otter announcement.

Beavers are the ones who carefully read
instruction manuals instead of throwing
them away.

"Honey, Mom and I are going to get you a swing
set this morning when the store opens, and you'll
be swinging by lunchtime!"

It was in fact lunchtime when I finally finished
putting together the three million bolts, screws, hex
nuts, flying ring washers and horizontal stabilizers
that came in the carton. Unfortunately, it was
lunchtime three weekends later! And while the
swing set was finally standing, it looked as if it had
just withstood a major earthquake and could fall
apart at any moment.

In classic otter fashion, the first thing I had done
after opening the box was to toss aside the instructions. After all, I reasoned, reading instructions
isn't fun. I knew it would be a snap putting the set
together. What almost snapped, however, was my
sanity as I "creatively" pounded and drilled new
holes to fit the parts that had obviously been
incorrectly shaped and drilled at the factory.

One last thing remained for me to do before
Cindy would trust our daughter's life to the
unusual-looking swing set I had created. I needed
to anchor it into the ground so that when several
children really got swinging, it wouldn't be pulled
over.

Once again, however, instead of doing things by
the instructions and anchoring it in concrete (as a
good beaver would have done), I opted for a

quicker and easier way. Namely, I bought four auger stakes to attach to each leg of the swing set. (Auger stakes are long, metal stakes that have a giant screw bit at one end.)

With a Herculean effort, I twisted each of the four stakes into the ground and then attached them to the swing set. At last it was finished, and Cindy gave Kari the green light to swing. She was swinging happily, and my creation actually looked as though it might work! But that's when I decided to do something funny while she was swinging through the air.

In Arizona, if you don't have some type of sprinkler system, you don't have grass. Thinking it would be entertaining, I walked over to the sprinkler box that was nearby to turn on the water for a moment.

I flipped the switch and—whoosh! Water began to spray all right, but not from the sprinkler heads. Instead, it was gushing out of the ground right where I had screwed in the auger stakes!

Had I stopped to check where the sprinkler lines were buried before anchoring the swing set? NO! Would a *beaver* have checked to see where the plastic pipes were buried before driving our long, metal spikes deep into the ground? Yes!

Kari escaped with her life from the geysers I had created, but the swing set didn't. It was in such bad shape, I finally had to break down and call—a beaver. My good friend Jim McGuire came over the next day and helped me reassemble the set and patch the sprinkler system—correctly.

What's the first thing he asked for? You guessed it! The directions! And this time, as if by magic, we actually did have Kari swinging by lunchtime, safe and dry.

For beavers, stress is reduced in the home or on the job by having a manual to follow. Unfortunately, life is often unpredictable, especially in marriage and parenting. Much of what happens in relationships falls outside the pages beavers have memorized. For example, a beaver mother may plan her family's weekend to the half hour. But if she lives with lions and otters, things can change by the *minute*, causing her no end of frustration.

We've seen beavers in counseling sessions be as firm as any lion, but for a different reason. They're not trying to win for the thrill of victory. Instead, they become hard on issues, and often on people, because they're so committed to doing what they think is right.

Beavers' natural strength of doing things right can make them God's quality control experts in a home. Held in balance, that can make them a very valuable addition to a family.

3. Beavers like to make careful decisions.

It was Christmas Eve, and I (Gary) was driving home when I saw the flags waving and the freshly painted sign that announced a new patio home complex had opened. The words "Immediate sale" and "Price reductions" caught my otter eyes and pulled me off the main road and up to the sales office.

After all, I thought, we had been in the same house for nine years. I had moved every year of my life growing up. With the kids getting older, we certainly didn't need all the room we had now. We were overdue for a change of address, and perhaps a patio home was just what we needed.

It was certainly just what the saleswoman thought I needed. She proceeded to make me an offer I was sure Norma couldn't refuse—until I talked to her about it.

"Gary," she said in her patient, softside voice, "we've talked about moving, but not into a patio home. What if something happens and Kari decides to move home instead of living in the dorm at school? What if Greg decides to come back home to finish school instead of staying at Oklahoma?"

"Ha!" I said. "Fat chance. The kids are perfectly happy where they are, and I would be if we could just get this patio home."

Norma is a real blend of personalities. She has a great deal of a characteristic we'll talk about later, golden retriever. But she also has many beaver traits. I guess that makes her a beaver-retriever.

In her systematic way, Norma's natural beaver instincts told her that this wasn't the place or time to move. There was too much uncertainty about where the kids would be living to change from a medium-sized, four-bedroom home to a small, three-bedroom patio home.

Beavers are good at thinking through all sides of an issue. They normally have excellent instincts when it comes to decision making, and they aren't afraid to say no. But they do have a weakness in that they can let the enthusiasm of others talk them out of their well-thought-out plans.

Over the course of the next few weeks, I took the kids to see the new condo we "needed" so much. It was bright and freshly painted, and soon their enthusiasm and mine were beginning to wear Norma down.

Finally, in her desire to please everyone, she dropped her arguments, and we all agreed to move into the new home. But still she said, "Gary, I think we're going to be sorry. This patio home is too small, and we're going to regret it!"

Sure enough, everything worked out just as Norma said it would. For the first few weeks, our new home fit Norma, Michael and me like a glove. But within three months, we needed two more fingers in the glove. Unexpectedly, we added two kids and had half as much space to put them in as in our former home.

Who would have known that just before Kari graduated, she would want to move back home with us? And who could have foreseen that Greg would decide to leave the University of Oklahoma and move back home to finish his college? My wife, the beaver, could and did.

I had used all my typical otter persuasion skills (more about that in chapter 6) to talk her into a decision that went against her natural grain. And once again, I learned I was wrong.

To take-charge lions and fast-paced otters, beavers can appear slow and overly cautious. Yet one of the great strengths they bring to a home is their ability to head off problems by saying no to bad decisions like the one I had made.

I finally listened to Norma's words of caution. Unfortunately, it was after we'd already bought the home. And after two years of putting up with cramped quarters, we finally moved back into a larger home just like our old one, except we had to pay more for it.

There are times when beavers can be so cautious that they fail to grasp an instant opportunity. One beaver husband we know could have bought a 1940 Cadillac convertible in mint condition for $2,000 from a business partner; the car eventually sold for more than ten times that amount at auction. But ninety-nine times out of a hundred, the beaver ability to make careful, thoughtful and correct decisions is a major strength.

4. Beavers like using their critical skills to solve problems.

The hardside ability to look at issues critically can be enormously valuable in problem solving. My (John's) "Aunt Dovie" demonstrated that truth vividly during World War II.

As the war raged in Europe and the Pacific, we had many heroes on the front lines. But there were also many hometown heroes who never got a medal and never went overseas. These were the men and women who rolled up their sleeves and went to work in defense plants that sprang up all over the country to support the war effort.

Aunt Dovie was one such woman. She stands all of five feet tall on a good day and probably weighs in at a little over ninety pounds. However, it was her beaver ability to take things apart that helped her track down a "Nazi saboteur" in the defense plant where she worked.

At Allison Division, General Motors, Indianapolis, they manufactured engines for the P-51 fighter plane—one of the most powerful fighters America provided her wartime pilots. The pistons of these engines were coated with silver, which was rationed and precious in 1944. My aunt was a section supervisor in the packing department.

As the pistons came off the production line, they went to packing, where they were immersed in oil, then heat-sealed in heavy-duty plastic wrap. Finally they were packed six to a prenumbered carton and shipped overseas to combat zones. As the supervisor in this area, Aunt Dovie was the last one to handle the pistons before they left for shipping. That's why she was one of the first people informed of a serious problem.

By the time the boxes of pistons arrived overseas and were opened, the silver plating was riddled with pinpoint holes!

The War Department wasted little time advising Allison, and the grapevine quickly began to buzz across the entire plant. The rumors raced from machine operator to machine operator. Foremen and supervisors began to cluster, holding somber discussions. "Pinpoint holes are showing up on the silver plate of our pistons. Engineering has called in the brass from Detroit. Quality control has tightened supervision of the plating department, but still the holes are showing up! There has to be someone—a saboteur—getting to the pistons at some point in the process."

Could someone be splashing acid on them somewhere on the production line? Or worse, in the final packing area? Would leaking the news at the plant be enough to flush out the culprit, or at least to make the saboteur fearful of further tampering?

That's when Aunt Dovie's beaver mind went to work. "G-men" trained to track down criminals were stationed in the plant. But never underestimate the power of a beaver when she starts taking problems apart!

Since my aunt was a supervisor as well as a beaver, she already knew every step of every job involved in inspecting and loading the pistons into packing cases. And in her determination to find the spy, she spent hours going through every possible place on the assembly line where acid could be applied. With her painstaking methods, she finally caught the perpetrator—or at least uncovered him.

It was lunchtime one day, and the break room at the factory was filled with people. Aunt Dovie was standing in line at the one snack machine they had. Suddenly, all her careful observations of every person in her department paid off. She saw the saboteur. Right before her was a culprit she never would have suspected. *It has to be!* she thought.

How obvious! She marveled at why she hadn't seen it sooner.

After the break, she watched closely as everyone who had been in line with her went right back to work. That's when her suspicions were confirmed. Without a doubt, she had found the traitor.

You see, the "Nazi spy" who had been pitting the silver plating wasn't using acid at all . . . but salt! The culprit was none other than—the peanut machine!

The workers would eat a handful of peanuts, then go right back to work without washing their hands. The salt left on their hands was eating through the soft silver plating as the pistons traveled overseas. Leave it to a beaver to see that something as small and seemingly insignificant as salted peanuts was actually *the* thing causing major problems.

Beavers love to go into detail. They enjoy reading maps and drawing up diagrams. The only problem is that besides being so good at taking things apart, they're also very good at taking apart *people* with whom they're upset.

If beavers respect and appreciate you, they can be as loyal as a golden retriever. However, if they're unhappy with you, they can use their perfectionistic bent to become piercing, hardside critics.

Like lions, beavers can communicate an inner intensity level. What's more, they, too, tend to keep others at a safe emotional distance, erecting an invisible barrier that people can sense nonetheless. And while they may not be as verbal as a lion, they can become just as hardside in their positions and hold just as firmly to what they think is right in a given situation.

Where do they get the motivation to do things in such an orderly, by-the-book manner? From their deep dislike of being wrong and their strong desire to do things right.

5. Beavers live by the motto "Let's do this right."

"If it's worth doing, it's worth doing right." Do you live by that country proverb? Are your socks all rolled up and color-coordinated instead of just being thrown in a drawer? Is your side of the closet so well organized that you can find everything you need to get dressed in the dark?

If so, you probably scored fairly high on the beaver scale. Doing things right, with precision and accuracy, is very important to a beaver.

We've given our personality test to several thousand people all across the country. And in each group we give the test to, the members of one profession consistently score at the top of the beaver scale. Who are they? Surgeons. Of course this makes sense. We would much rather have a beaver surgeon operating on us, making sure everything was done just right, than a fun-loving otter surgeon who was more concerned about having a great time in the operating room!

This natural strength of spotting things that are wrong and wanting to make them right heads off many mistakes. We know of one mother who pushed this natural strength to an extreme, however, and made a major mistake with her son.

"We miss you, Son, and we love you," the voice on the phone said.

"Thanks, Dad. I miss you too," Roger said.

"And Son, one more thing. Could you spare the time to write your mother? I know it would encourage her."

Roger's father wasn't trying to be pushy. He knew that his wife and son had corresponded regularly when their boy first went away to an out-of-state college. She was genuinely interested in hearing about his life at school, and he could see that she loved getting his letters. But her son's letters had gradually come less and less frequently, and finally not at all.

Little did Roger's mother know that she was doing something to close his spirit and block his desire to write to her. She never would have dreamed that a common beaver characteristic was affecting her son the way it was.

There was a long pause on the other end of the phone before Roger spoke again. With emotion in his voice, he told his father, "Dad, I'm not writing Mom anymore. If she wants to talk to me, I'll talk to her over the phone."

"But why?" his father asked, obviously confused.

With a deep sigh, Roger said, "Because I'm sick of sending her letters and then getting them back with the spelling corrected. I've got enough people grading my papers here at school and giving me a hard time. I don't need to feel like a failure every time I write her a letter."

Roger's mother deeply loved her son. But her beaver tendency to do things right and be hard on even minor mistakes meant that if there was any kind of error in a letter, she just *had* to mention it. For her, it was only making wrong things right. But for her sensitive, golden retriever son, every red mark crossed out his feelings of being loved and accepted, not just the spelling mistakes on the page.

Every company and family needs a beaver. But like lions, beavers can get so wrapped up in the results of a project that they fail to see how dramatically they affect those working or living with them. Beavers need to make sure the details of a project or a letter don't become so important that they miss the message and people behind it. Without realizing it, they can come across extremely hard. The worst damage beavers do, however, is often to themselves.

6. Beavers tend to turn anger inward.

Out of all the animals in the family zoo, beavers are the most prone to times of depression and associated physical problems. Why? The reason can be found in the meaning of depression itself: anger turned inward.

While lions roar when they're angry and otters verbally attack, beavers tend to turn their anger on themselves. What usually fans the flames of their anger? Making mistakes.

Danny was only nine when his parents noticed a

serious problem that was surprising in light of the strong beaver instincts he had exhibited since toddlerhood. While the other children in the family would throw their clothes and shoes in the closet, his shoes were always lined up and his little hangers hung in neat rows. He brushed his teeth carefully each night, while his otter brother usually just ran his toothbrush under the faucet so their mother would think he had brushed.

When school started, Danny always got high marks on his homework, and especially on citizenship—that is, until he reached the fourth grade.

A few months into the new academic year, Danny was struggling with school. He was withdrawing from friends and even beginning to shut out family members. He would sit for hours in his room with the door closed, ostensibly studying. But still his grades were suffering, and his attitude toward school was getting worse. He even began to fake illness to avoid having to go to class. And this from a boy who had nearly perfect attendance in the past.

What could bring such dramatic changes in only a few months? Danny had run into something no beaver can live with consistently without showing negative effects.

Mr. Ryan, Danny's teacher, was well liked by most of the parents and children. He had played pro football for one year and was a strong believer in challenging his students to do their best in sports and in the classroom. But there was one problem.

What proved motivating to many students was emotionally killing Danny.

As we've mentioned, beavers like to have clear directions and to be able to ask informational questions. But there's something else they need as well: they need to feel a strong sense of support and be in a *noncritical atmosphere* to do their best work.

Mr. Ryan's way of challenging his students was to confront them. He knew Danny was a top student. So to motivate him, he would stand over him in the classroom and push him to do his best work. He would take mistakes Danny and others made and parade them in front of everyone.

While the teacher always smiled when he challenged Danny, this shy beaver youngster never saw any humor in his teacher's methods. All he felt was incredible pressure to be perfect so he could avoid being humiliated in front of his classmates.

It's important to understand that both golden retrievers and beavers tend to slow down under pressure. In fact, increasing the pressure on most beavers is like turning down the gas on the water heater when you want hot water.

As Danny became more afraid of failing, he started going slower to make sure he wouldn't make a mistake. As a result, the coach was constantly pushing him to go faster. "Come on, Danny," he'd say as he handed out an in-class assignment. "You're smart. You can finish this in twenty minutes."

Left on his own—or even better, with gentle encouragement and the freedom to ask questions

—Danny *could* have finished in ten minutes. But faced with the pressure of loud challenges and the constant fear of having his mistakes pointed out in front of the class, he was taking twenty minutes just to read the instructions!

"I don't understand what it takes to motivate your son," Mr. Ryan told Danny's parents at the first parent-teacher conference. That was an understatement. While he saw the problem lying with their "unmotivated son," it was actually a reflection of his lack of understanding of the best way to motivate a beaver child.

Beavers need to learn that it's all right to fail and that it's healthy to call for help when they're struggling.

Danny needed the calm reassurance and opendoor policy that had always been there with his previous teachers. When he didn't get them, he didn't call out to Mom and Dad for help the way an otter child would. He didn't turn around and fight back like a lion. He was too intimidated to express his hurt and frustration toward the coach. What did that leave?

The only safe person to attack was himself. And in the short space of a semester, he had taken himself apart so many times that his self-confidence was in shambles. A former A student, he was now fully convinced that he was stupid and a failure, and he was heading right into a deep juvenile depression.

Parents of beaver children need to make sure they praise and encourage their children's character as well as their accomplishments. They also need to protect their children's character. And they can do that by taking the pressure off their kids to feel that life is only worth living if they get 100 percent right on every test.

Beavers need to learn that it's all right to fail and that it's healthy to call for help when they're struggling. Also, if there are other people in the home (particularly otters or lions), beavers need to guard against assuming that everyone will see the same problems or in the same way as they do.

For example, a broken slat on a wooden fence in the backyard might really bother a beaver. After all, someone might look in or, even worse, break in. But most otters, not being as detail-oriented, would probably have to see an entire section of the fence fall down before it caught their attention!

Finally, parents who are beavers need to value those children whose natural temperaments tend toward having a sock *room* instead of a sock drawer. That's not to say that parents shouldn't hand out chores, give room inspections, and expect their children to learn responsibility.[1] But with the average child requiring two to three hundred reminders before finally building a task into a habit, it's important that beaver parents allow their children to fail at something without considering themselves failures as parents.

Fortunately, Danny's story had a happy ending. Mr. Ryan was always teachable as a player, and he also had the wisdom to be teachable as a teacher. After his talk with Danny's parents, he learned what Danny needed to excel. Mr. Ryan decreased the hardside motivation and increased his softside support—more encouragement, more details on the homework or in-class assignments, more spontaneous hugs, and no more public displays of criticism.

We can help the beavers in our homes, offices and classrooms to feel more successful if we'll keep in mind their inner sensitivity to criticism. Being soft with them while hard on their problems is a must.

7. Beavers tend to focus on the past.

As a well-organized beaver, young Diane spent a great deal of time planning her future life. And for nearly thirty years, things went pretty much according to script.

She attended the college she had chosen years in advance and married a wonderful young man after graduation, just as she'd always planned. They saved enough money to put a down payment on a house, and then, after four years of "just we two," along came her first child—born only one day from the due date.

Like her mother, Diane got pregnant easily and had no problems carrying the baby—just as she'd expected. But then something hit her that greatly troubles many beavers: the *unexpected.*

Two years had passed since the birth of her son, and in Diane's mind, it was time for her little boy to have a little sister. But as weeks turned into months and then a year of trying and waiting, she finally had to face the possibility of infertility, and it knocked her well-ordered world out of its carefully planned path.

Diane would have scored near the top on the beaver scale. She took great comfort in following the same path her parents had. But now, for the first time, it was as if she had lost her map. Month after month she tried to get pregnant, and finally she broke down and went to a medical specialist. After that, there were the tests, the shots, the medications, the waiting and always the tears.

A beaver's primary time frame is the past. Beavers want a track record. They like knowing how something has been done before. And if it works, they'll stay with it. Beavers also tend to look to the past as a way of explaining present situations or problems.

Diane lay in bed for hours at a time, searching the past for some secret sin that could have brought on such a personal calamity. A hundred times a day, she would slam herself emotionally for not "starting my family earlier" or "not knowing" what she couldn't possibly have known.

Caught in the grasp of "What if . . ." she was no longer free to enjoy her son or her husband, David, who deeply loved her. What's more, she couldn't enjoy her relationship with God anymore.

Her husband tried to encourage her by reading Bible verses on faith like this one in the book of

Hebrews: "Faith is being sure of what we hope for and certain of what we do not see."[2]

"Honey, just have faith," he'd say. "We'll get pregnant."

For her otter husband, picturing a positive future was second nature. (More about that in chapter 6.) The future was where he spent most of his time anyway. But almost by biblical definition, faith is more of a challenge for a beaver.

Faith focuses on the future. As the book of Hebrews puts it, faith is the assurance of things hoped for. It involves giving over all control of something important to someone else and still feeling positive about it. What pulled Diane through the three and a half years when she struggled with life's being "out of control" until God brought her another child by adoption?

"To be honest," she said, "I couldn't look into the future and feel as positive about things as David did. But I could look *back* at all the times God has been faithful to me in the past and draw strength from them."

Diane turned the corner in this faith-stretching time when she was finally able to use her beaver bent toward focusing on the past as an ally, not as an enemy to blast herself. Her faith in the present wasn't made stronger by trying to become a visionary like her husband. Rather, faith came by using her natural strength as a historian to bring reassurance that God indeed knew the best direction for her life.

We've now seen seven character traits that consistently show up in the lives of our beaver friends.

1. Beavers keep a close watch on their emotions.
2. Beavers actually read instruction books.
3. Beavers like to make careful decisions.
4. Beavers like using their critical skills to solve problems.
5. Beavers live by the motto "Let's do it right!"
6. Beavers often turn anger inward.
7. Beavers tend to focus on the past.

All seven of these characteristics help make these people exceptional employees, friends and family members. What's more, our Lord Himself had beaver traits. For example, did Christ like to do things "by the book"? Absolutely. In fact, He only did what was right and in His Father's will. Not one jot or tittle of God's law did He ignore.

Beavers have many great strengths, but like our lion friends, they can drift away from a healthy balance point. Without realizing it, they can let their personality or past push them into a hardside way of relating to others.

We've seen that a sensitive lion and a balanced beaver are among the most helpful, sought-after animals on this planet. But if they don't learn to add softness to their lives, their relationships often end up on the endangered species list.

If you have any lion or beaver characteristics in your life, be sure to read the next chapters that describe our otter and golden retriever friends. But you'll also get a great deal out of chapters 10 and 11, where we'll give you ten specific ways to add a healthy softness to your love.

Next up is a look at the third animal in the family zoo, a specialist at having fun, being creative, motivating others—and getting kids to wear cereal!

6

Discovering the Strengths
of an Otter

Have you ever seen otters in the wild or in a zoo? Everything they do seems related in one way or another to having fun. Sea otters even eat by floating on their backs while they balance their food on their stomach. How do their human counterparts act? Much the same way. People who score high on the otter scale are parties waiting to happen.

We've seen that the overriding drive for a lion is to conquer and accomplish something, and the major strength of a beaver is to do things right and in a quality way. We've also seen that left unchecked, they both tend to move toward the hard side of love. But the driving motivation for soft-sided otters is to have fun and enjoy life! That's just one of seven characteristics otters tend to share.

1. Otters just want to have fun.

If there's a way to have fun doing something, you can expect an otter to try it. We're both purebred otters, which probably explains the "funny" idea I (John) had one day.

When my daughter Kari Lorraine was two years old, she loved eating with her hands. Like many little ones, she tended to mash her food into unique shapes before eating it. And it was her lack of dining etiquette that got this otter into trouble one Sunday morning.

Time was running out in our race to get to church at least stylishly late. (Otters *enjoy* being stylishly late.) Kari and I were still sitting at the table, eating breakfast and watching "Sesame Street." I had poured her a small bowl full of a multivitamin cereal that should be renamed Post Soggies. The moment milk hits the flakes, they instantly turn into mush—the ideal thing for Kari to play in.

Picking up a handful of this glop, she let the milk run through her fingers. After squishing the cereal about a dozen times, she finally tired of the game and turned to me to ask, "Daddy, what do I do with this now?"

Ask a fun-loving otter what to do with soggy cereal? "Sweetheart," I said with a straight face, "you need to put it on your nose."

Was that a good thing to say to a two-year-old?

If there's a way to have fun doing
something, you can expect an otter to try it.

Instantly her eyes lit up, and without hesitation,
she broke into a big smile and smashed the cereal
right into her face. We were both laughing hysteri-
cally when she reached down and—*pow*—mashed
another handful all over her nose.

I should have been in control of the situation.
Instead, I was laughing and rolling on the floor. We
even went through a second bowl of cereal just so
we could laugh some more at the incredible mess
we'd created.

Two full bowls of soggy cereal and milk were all
over us and the table. Cracker, the dog, was getting
sick from slurping up this unexpected treat. And
that's when Cindy walked into the room . . . and
saw brown slime everywhere.

Cindy is a fun-loving person, but she's a beaver, and off-the-wall humor is not the goal of
her life. Ten minutes before we were supposed to
be at church, instead of being in the car, we were
outside hosing down Kari and trying to get the
breakfast nook cleaned up enough so we could
leave.

Already I could tell I was in trouble, but it was
the rest of the story that really sealed my fate.

My wife gently pulled me aside after we had
dropped Kari off at her room at church. "John,"
she said, "you shouldn't teach her to play with her

food that way. I work with her all week to teach her livable table manners for a two-year-old, and then you give her the green light to wipe out the kitchen!"

"Honey," I said good-naturedly, "lighten up." (*Lighten up* is a standard otter phrase meaning "Let's not get serious. Let's just have fun!") In my mind, I had experienced a great time of laughter and bonding with my daughter. But like many otters, I had forgotten a fundamental principle. Namely, we need to think through the consequences of our "fun" behavior.

After church, we were with some good friends (thankfully) at a local restaurant for lunch. Our food had just arrived, and we'd managed to get all the kids quieted down to say grace. We had just finished praying when I looked up and my heart sank.

There was Kari, a huge smile on her face and a massive lump of spaghetti in her hands. In my quest for fun, I had failed to consider that two-year-olds tend to repeat what they've learned— especially when it's gotten such a tremendous, positive response at breakfast.

"No!" I tried to say, but it was too late. Our entire section of the restaurant came unglued as the people watched my two-year-old wearing her spaghetti dinner and me trying to melt under the table. The look on my wife's face told me I was the one who had acted like a two-year-old. (It wasn't the first time I'd seen that look.)

If you're the parent of otters, expect them to

come up with fun and creative ways to eat their food, take a bath, or do their homework. Marriage to an otter means getting used to surprises, spontaneity, and seeing a one-hour project in the yard turn into a three-hour, fun-filled adventure.

Beavers and golden retrievers appreciate and seek out an otter's fun-loving attitude. But it can become a source of frustration later in a relationship when they ask, "Do you *ever* get serious?"

Otters need to realize that while keeping things light is generally fine, they can't do it all the time. Avoiding serious discussions is like forcing their mates to live on a steady diet of icing instead of a complete meal of meaningful communication. Sometimes otters, too, have to tackle difficult topics and, especially, go deeper in relationships than light, surface-level humor. In short, that's why they need the ability to tap into the hard side of love.

My otter escapade with Kari produced little more than hurt feelings for me and the need for a new wardrobe for Kari. But there was a time for Gary when another otter characteristic nearly turned a fun time into a tragedy.

2. Otters are great at motivating others to action.

We Smalleys have enjoyed camping for years, and that's what led us to the beautiful, forested California Sierra mountains. At one place we stopped was a small waterfall. It would have been rushing with water in the spring, but this was late August, and the flow had slowed to a trickle.

The water didn't fall over a sheer cliff but down a

steeply sloping hill. As I (Gary) climbed toward the top, I could see that the moss had formed a soft, slippery, green carpet that seemed to make a natural slide down to the pool below. That's when I had a great otter idea.

If I could get Greg, my older son, to climb to the top of the waterfall and slide down into the big pool, I could take the action shot of a lifetime. I was sure my new camera would capture just the right picture that would end up on the cover of our family album.

"Greg, come up here," I yelled down to where the rest of the family was seated at the base of the waterfall. He quickly climbed to where I was, halfway to the top, and I explained my idea to him.

"Dad," he said skeptically, looking at the slope and distance involved, "are you sure I won't get going too fast and miss that curve down there on my way to the pool?"

As I looked to where he was pointing, I could see what he meant. The slide went down a fairly straight path until the last possible moment. There it angled to the left before dropping into the deep water below.

"Trust me," I said. (*Trust me* is another classic otter saying that means "Don't ask me questions as if you think I've actually thought through all the details. It'll work out. Let's just go for it!")

"Greg," I said, "if it will make you feel any better, I'll position myself right where the slide turns so I can catch you if need be." Actually, I was thinking that from that position, I could get a great shot of him coming down the slide, and then I could turn around and get an incredible picture of him falling into the water.

I could see, however, that my words didn't make my son feel much better. But otters can be awfully convincing, and I kept talking. Before long, off he went to the top of the falls and the ride of his life.

With many accidents, things happen so fast that they seem to go at a speed all their own. Through my camera lens, I saw Greg push off the top, begin sliding down the hill, and pick up momentum. The grade was much steeper than I had realized (having never climbed all the way to the top), and before he had gone halfway down the hill, he was already traveling much too fast.

I gave up trying to focus my camera and started to put it down so I could catch Greg when—*zoom* —he shot right by me before I could even move. Need I say, he never made the turn! Instead of falling into the pool below, he bounced down the hill and disappeared over a small cliff!

As I turned, I saw Norma's face below. Her eyes were open wide with terror, and she screamed as she saw what I couldn't see yet. I ran to the edge of the cliff, and as I looked down, I watched Greg bouncing off rocks and finally lying still at the bottom of the hill.

My first thought was, *I've killed my son!* As

I scrambled down the hill, I couldn't believe what I'd done. *Why didn't I think this through? Why did I talk him into it?* I scolded myself over and over.

Thankfully, this story has a happy ending. By the time I reached the bottom, Greg was already sitting up. He was slightly shaken, but he had kept his head when he first hit the ground and had slid on his seat until he came to a stop.

It was beaver/retriever Mom who was shaken up the most. In fact, we were going through some old family pictures recently and came across slides of that infamous waterfall trip. Norma leaned over to me and said, "Gary, that's the one time in my life when if I could have reached you, there's no telling what I would have done to you!"

Otters are excellent motivators. They can captivate an audience or encourage someone who is fainthearted. Many otters use their verbal skills to become preachers or teachers. And all of them seem to have a natural gift of gab that can provide a home or office with extra energy and drive.

3. Otters tend to avoid the fine print.

As a single parent, my (John's) mother played "Mr. Dad" in many ways, taking my brother and me camping and encouraging us in sports. But one thing we did miss out on was learning the skills of using tools.

Otters are excellent motivators. They can
captivate an audience or encourage someone
who is fainthearted.

My lack of mechanical abilities was never a
major issue until I got married. That's when my
Cindy discovered how unmechanical I am and
began to encourage me to improve in that area.

I'll never forget (or live down!) one incident. We
were sitting at home, watching television, when a
commercial came on for a particular brand of
motor oil. As a novel twist, the commercial fea-
tured a trained monkey changing the oil to show
you how easy it was. The monkey unscrewed the oil
plug underneath, took off the old filter and put on a
new one, then poured in fresh oil. "What could be
simpler?" the commercial implied.

"John," Cindy said with a smile, "I'll bet you
could go out and change the oil in our car after
seeing that!"

Change the oil . . . I thought. "You bet I could!" I
said, and I jumped up from my chair, enthusiastic
about saving us major dollars and protecting the
engine like never before. As it turned out, the car
should have had someone protecting it from me.

I was motivated (one otter characteristic), and I
was ready to have fun (a second), but did I read any
instructions before setting out to change the oil for
the first time? No (our third otter trait).

Not having any tools, I went next door and
borrowed a neighbor's wrench. With that, I was all

set. I got under the car with my plastic pan ready to catch the old oil, and I managed to unscrew a large bolt that looked as if it was right beneath the engine. As soon as I removed the bolt, out came a gush of red oil.

Red oil? I thought to myself. *It's a good thing I decided to change this stuff. When oil gets old, it must turn really red, just like this.*

After letting all the "oil" run out, I replaced the bolt, put in the six or seven quarts of oil I'd bought (*After all,* I thought, *it's a big engine*), and was ready to go. Right? Wrong. I was ready to ruin the car.

If you haven't guessed already, I had unknowingly drained out all the transmission fluid, not the oil! I now had about twelve quarts of oil in the car instead of five, and not one drop of transmission fluid.

When did we make this exciting discovery? That night as we drove the car—when the transmission burned up in the middle of the Central Expressway in Dallas.

While my experience with avoiding details sent us to the transmission shop, in many cases an otter's ability to operate without instructions provides much more positive results. For example, many chefs, artists and musicians are otters who use their natural ability to "wing it" to create works of art. Trust otters to come up with an innovative way of doing something, but trust them to rarely do it by the book.

Otters share a fourth character trait as well. It

seems that God has built within them an emotional escape elevator that can lift them above all but the most serious problems, a characteristic wrapped up in their view of time.

4. Otters focus on the future.

Otters rarely think problems are as serious as others seem to think, and that can be a real advantage. Why? Because otters tend to be incredibly optimistic, a trait that springs primarily from their view of time and can help keep them soft, even in trials.

For the average otter, the future is inseparably linked to the present. It's a view of life that easily looks down the road. And since 99 percent of all problems exist either in the past or the present, focusing on the future, where everything can still work out, helps them stay optimistic.

We recently read a story that demonstrates beautifully the value of such optimism. It was the gripping account of an American pilot who was shot down by the North Vietnamese, captured, and imprisoned in the "Hanoi Hilton" for several years. We were fascinated to read about the skill many prisoners developed to cope with their confinement by mentally setting aside today's problems and focusing on tomorrow.[1]

In the confines of prison, these men designed and built homes and other structures all in their minds, even to the point of moving furniture into the rooms. Others set up imaginary baseball or football leagues, complete with regional rivalries, playoffs and college drafts. The ability to use the imagination to focus on the future helped them to face their present trials.

That same skill is consistently seen in otter individuals as well. Jean's daughter was born with a genetic birth defect. For many parents, little Diane's physical limitations would have looked like a closed door to a special future. But as an otter mother, Jean tapped into her natural strengths and lifted her eyes beyond that immediate barrier.

In faith, Jean kept believing and encouraging her daughter to become more than anyone else thought she could be. It took years of everyday hard work, but Diane eventually blossomed beyond everyone else's expectations because of her mother's ability to focus on a future goal.

The problem was that Diane's left arm had never developed below the elbow. At birth, only a fleshy appendage was present where her forearm and hand should have been. But her otter mother kept focusing on the future and telling her, "You can do anything you want."

All through grade school and high school, Jean stood beside Diane, encouraging her and instilling optimism. Then came college, and Diane decided to major in music at a very fine school in central Texas. The picture her mother had always given her of a positive future made her feel she really *could* do anything she set her mind to—even take piano as a minor, as all music students were required to do.

The happiest and proudest person at Diane's senior recital was her otter mother, someone who used her personal strengths to encourage and enrich the life of her daughter.

Optimistically focusing on the future can be a natural advantage, but it can be a weakness as well. That's especially true if otters push their natural strength out of balance and end up ignoring or explaining away their problems. That was clearly illustrated by one couple who came into our office for counseling.

Ray and Rochelle had been married for only a few weeks when they decided to divorce. In their minds, they had given the relationship a good shot. But before they actually filed papers, someone convinced them to come in for counseling.

The young man was an off-the-chart otter. Can you guess what he would say about all their problems? With his focus on the future, he'd been saying things to her like, "Just give it some more time." "Things are bound to get better." "Next month, you'll see." "Honey, give me a chance."

Unfortunately, Rochelle looked at life from the opposite vantage point. As an off-the-chart beaver, she focused on the past. She'd hear his pleas that the future would be different, but she wanted to see a history of success before she would believe it. And because things hadn't been good for the past six weeks or in the many months before their wedding, she made statements like, "It hasn't gotten any better yet" and "Our courtship was miserable, so why should I believe things are going to improve?"

Ray had failed in his courtship promise to change some habits Rochelle hated, and he minimized her growing feelings of despair after they were married. He had to realize in a hurry that in his situation, the future alone didn't hold the key to keeping his marriage together. It was only when he woke up to the harsh realities of the present and a wife who was about to leave him that he finally changed his focus.

Fortunately, they made it through counseling, and at last check, through five years of marriage. But they've both learned something vital about time. Namely, conflicting views of time in a marriage have to be addressed. The more an otter can respect the need other personalities have for a track record, the better.

Held in balance, otters' optimism based on a future focus is healthy. It can help build a positive outlook for themselves and others. But as you might imagine, their fun-loving, upbeat outlook on life can make it very difficult for them to face confrontation.

5. Otters tend to avoid confrontation at all costs.

As a newlywed, Dan was thrilled with both his new wife, Nanci, and his new job. At last he had been promoted to the very position he wanted in the advertising department of his company. He couldn't dream of things' being any better. He was right. Things were about to become a whole lot worse.

Dan had heard rumors of a hostile takeover of his company, but those rumors had been flying around for years. Then one day, people ran down the hallways, shouting out the news that they had been bought by a multinational corporation.

Dan told Nanci about the takeover. But he put off telling her the whole story: the new owners had their own ad agency, and it was very likely that his services would no longer be needed.

Dan wasn't trying to hurt Nanci. Just the opposite. With his soft way of handling problems, he thought he was doing the right thing in sparing her from knowing what "might" happen. But his interest in protecting her wasn't the only reason he didn't tell her. By not talking about his job problems with his bride, he put off facing them himself, at least for a short time.

Unfortunately, time ran out for Dan the day Nanci beat him home and found his pink slip in the mail!

If you scored high on the otter scale, expect to struggle at times with confronting others or tackling difficult discussions that demand a hardside stance. The guidelines in the chapters on adding a healthy hard side to your love (chapters 10 and 11) will help you gain the balance you need in this area.

That's not to say that all otters will become manipulative or deceptive like Dan to avoid confrontation. But most otters are prone to avoiding explosive issues or procrastinating on having those hard discussions that aren't any fun.

6. Otters are tremendous networkers.

The sixth common characteristic of otters is one that makes them great employees or helpful friends. Namely, they seem blessed with the ability to put people together with other people.

Otters rarely meet a stranger. They know people who know people who know people. The only problem is that they don't remember everybody's name! They meet so many people, soon everyone they see can become "Old Buddy" or "Sweetheart."

My (Gary's) daughter, Kari Lynn, has a lot of otter in her and is one of the world's great networkers. At the time of this writing, she's in her first year of teaching at an inner-city school that historically has had poor attendance at parent-teacher meetings.

Rather than sit back and hope things might go better with her class, Kari took the initiative to schedule, on her own, a first-of-the-year potluck dinner for her students' families. And more than sixty people showed up!

What Kari had done is something most otters can do in a heartbeat—get people together for an event. She had heard about the low turnouts, but that didn't stop her. She knew that if she began calling the parents, and if she added the drawing card of food, anything could happen. And with all her phone networking and mentioning that so and so was bringing this, and so and so was bringing that, she had everyone from grandmothers to uncles come to get acquainted and enjoy dinner.

The principal was so impressed by Kari's enthusiasm for getting parents involved that he immediately asked her to help the PTA president plan several parent meetings throughout the school year.

We've seen that otters have many natural softside skills that can easily translate into friendships and fun relationships. But there's one problem these members of the family zoo share as well, and parents of otter children need to be aware of it.

Take the otters' deep need to be liked by everyone and be part of the group. Mix in their impulsive, creative tendencies with their love of excitement and adventure. Altogether you've got the perfect recipe for the personality that's most vulnerable to peer pressure.

7. Otters are very susceptible to peer pressure.

There's a man in the Old Testament who definitely lacked the playfulness of an otter but otherwise seemed to have many otter characteristics. Unfortunately, they were almost all pushed out of balance to the point of being weaknesses, not strengths.

When the Israelites demanded a king like all their neighbor nations, Saul was selected. Like many otters, he was concerned with how things looked to others. He was a head taller than anyone else and extremely attractive. But Israel's focus on the external in looking for a king compelled Samuel the prophet to say, "Man looks at the outward appearance, but the Lord looks at the heart."[2]

Saul also liked to be in the spotlight, particularly out in front of his troops. However, in typical otter fashion, he didn't think through the details of all the orders he gave his men. In fact, he once gave an impulsive order that none of his soldiers was to eat or drink during a major battle, and it cost Israel a great victory and nearly the life of Saul's son.

Under pressure, Saul reacted by attacking verbally those around him (something otters tend to do). But perhaps worst of all, he was terribly concerned with popular opinion. In fact, he was more concerned with being a people-pleaser than with pleasing God.[3]

Unfortunately, King Saul gave in to peer pressure and directly disobeyed God by letting his troops keep some of the loot from a major conquest. And as a result of his actions, God tore the kingdom from his hands.

None of us will lose a kingdom because we cave in to peer pressure. But that doesn't mean we won't lose someone's respect, a job or even our children to drugs or alcohol. And parents of otters need to make sure they build a strong friendship with their children to help them through the difficult times of adolescence, when peer pressure is so strong.[4]

Otters make popular leaders and personalities. However, they would do well to remember that the condition of the heart counts most, not the number of friends they have or how well they're liked.

Otters find it easy to be soft on people. What

often is not so easy is being hard on problems. And the dangers of being a people-pleaser should be kept in mind amidst the fun, energy and excitement otters create.

In review, we've looked at seven traits otters tend to share:

1. Otters just want to have fun.
2. Otters are great at motivating others to action.
3. Otters avoid the fine print.
4. Otters focus on the future.
5. Otters avoid confrontation at all costs.
6. Otters are tremendous networkers.
7. Otters are very susceptible to peer pressure.

Otters aren't the only animals that have a natural softside bent. As you turn the page, you'll discover another group of people who tend to have an incredible capacity for deep, long-lasting relationships.

They're the ones with the sign on the forehead saying, "I like you. I'll be a great friend." Their nonverbal cues tell everyone they see, "Call me; I'd love to listen to you for hours." They're the ones who seem to come equipped with the most natural softside characteristics: our golden retriever friends.

7

Discovering the Strengths
of a Golden Retriever

Several years ago, I (John) served as the staff counselor at a large church. After seeing numerous couples, I began to realize you can tell a great deal about people simply by watching the way they walk into the counseling office. When Dale and Diane first shuffled in and then stiffened as I pointed for them to sit on the same couch, I knew their marriage was in big trouble.

"Well," I said, looking at their forms and letting them get seated as far apart as they could without falling off the couch. "It says here that you've been married for twenty-eight years. That's quite an accomplishment. It also says you're really struggling right now." Looking up from reading their case notes, I asked, "How long have things been rough?"

They glanced at each other as if looking for permission to speak, then turned and said in unison, "Twenty-eight years!"

Without ever giving them our personality test, I knew instantly that at least one of them was a golden retriever. Why? Because of all the animals in the family zoo, golden retrievers can absorb the most emotional pain and still maintain their commitment to another person.

How do they do this? By possessing at least seven God-given characteristics that plant them squarely on the soft side of love—qualities like making loyalty a top priority regardless of the personal cost.

1. Above all, golden retrievers are loyal.

The year was 1864, and in Edinburgh, Scotland, lived an old man named Jock. For years he had been a faithful shepherd, braving the elements and protecting his flocks. But the rugged highland hills had taken their toll. At nearly seventy years of age, he still had the skill and heart of a shepherd, but not the health. His legs could no longer make the climb to gather in a stray or chase off a predator. And though the family he worked for loved him, finances were so tight that they couldn't keep him on any longer. So, hobbled on the outside and hurting inside, he rode in a bouncing wagon from his heartland to his new home in the city.

Once there, Jock turned into a handyman and

made many friends of the city's merchants. They liked Old Jock for his warm smile and needed him for his workman's skills. He was a wizard at odd jobs like fixing an unfixable chair and caulking a window so the wet, Scottish cold couldn't rush through a crack. But for all his friends, his family included only one: an orphan Skye terrier he had adopted by the name of Bobby.

Of all the animals in the family zoo, golden retrievers can absorb the most emotional pain and still maintain their commitment to another person.

Jock and Bobby were inseparable as they made their way past the various shops, looking for work. Their routine was always the same. They began their day at a local restaurant where there was a small job in exchange for a warm meal. Then they'd make their way down the street, with a stop in each establishment to see if there was a need for the tinker's trade. Finally, at night, the two of them would go back to a run-down flophouse that served as their home.

It's said that many people have a feeling, or inner knowledge, when their time to die is near. And so it was for Jock. More than a year had come and gone since the old Scotsman had come to the city. Now it was late summer, and the heather was in full bloom in the hills. As the sun came up one day, instead of walking down to the restaurant with Bobby, he pushed his bed next to the only window in the room. There he lay, looking up to the towering hills and his beloved Scottish highland.

"Laddie," he said, stroking Bobby's thick, black hair with a hand that now held only the strength of love in it, "it's time for me to go home. They'll no be making me leave the countryside again. I'm sorry, lad, but you'll be having to find your own way in life now."

Only someone who has truly loved another could know how deep was the bond between these two. As the dying shepherd looked into the eyes of his closest friend, his own grew clouded. A chill swept over him, and Bobby, the little, black dog, snuggled closer to his master. He did his best to keep him warm one last time as old Jock slipped from life to eternity.

Jock was buried the next day in an unusual place for a pauper. Because of where he died and the need to inter the body quickly, he was laid to rest in one of Edinburgh's finest graveyards, Greyfriar's Churchyard. Amidst the mighty and most noble of Scottish history, a common man was entombed. But that's just where the story begins.

The next morning, little Bobby showed up at the same restaurant he and Jock had visited every morning. Then he made his rounds of the shops, just as he and Jock always had. This continued day after day. But somehow, Bobby would disappear at night, only to be back at the restaurant the next morning.

Concerned friends of Old Jock wondered where the dog was sleeping, until at last the mystery was revealed. Each night, Bobby didn't look for the warmth of a fireplace, or even for a shelter from the biting Scottish wind and rain. He snuck into Greyfriar's cemetery to take up his position on his master's grave.

The caretaker of the cemetery would chase off the dog whenever he saw him. After all, there was a city ordinance against dogs in cemeteries. He tried fixing the fence and even putting up booby traps to catch the dog. Finally, with the help of a local constable, little Bobby was caught and impounded for not having a license. Since no one could claim legal ownership of him, it looked as if Bobby would have to be destroyed.

Friends of Old Jock and Bobby who heard of his plight actually filed suit on Bobby's behalf in the local court. Finally, the day arrived when their case came before the high tribunal in Edinburgh.

It would take nothing short of a miracle to save Bobby's life, not to mention making it possible for this faithful dog to stay near his friend's grave. That's exactly what happened, however, as an act unparalleled in Scottish history took place.

Before the judge could pass sentence, a horde of children from the streets came rushing into the courtroom. Penny by penny, these urchins had raised the seven shillings needed for a license for Bobby.

The lord provost was so impressed by the children's love for the animal that he officially gave the dog the "Freedom of the City," making him city property, with a special collar declaring this fact.

Now Bobby could run freely, playing with the children during the day. But each night, *for the 14 years until he died in 1879,* a loyal, loving friend kept his silent sentinel in Greyfriar's graveyard, right next to his master's side. Should you ever visit Edinburgh, you can visit the statue of Greyfriar's Bobby that's still in the old churchyard, more than 110 years since he died.[1]

Greyfriar's Bobby demonstrated something that comes naturally to the human members of the family zoo who score high on the golden retriever scale. In them you see the loyalty to stay at someone's bedside, to listen to others' problems for hours at a time, to lend a helping hand even on a Saturday or holiday.

That incredible kind of softside love and loyalty is being given in many homes today where golden retriever husbands and wives care for their families.

We think of Brenda, who held on for five and a half years while her husband was a prisoner of war in Vietnam and never once gave up loving and praying for him. Then there's Charlie, a rugged outdoorsman who hasn't been fishing in years as he takes care of his invalid wife's needs.

But golden retriever loyalty isn't seen only in dramatic examples like these. Many husbands and wives are unsung heroes, making strong loyalty to their families, their companies and their churches a hallmark of their relationships. What a strength that kind of loyalty is!

As we'll see in a later chapter, however, golden retrievers' deep loyalty can have a dark side as well. Terms like *codependency* and *negative enabler* can be laid at the feet of those who, in the name of loyalty, push their strengths into weakness.

Loyalty is the predominant characteristic of a golden retriever person, and in many ways, it acts like an umbrella above them all. Yet underneath that trait are six others that are just as important. The first we'll look at is a close cousin to loyalty. Springing from the retriever's strong sense of commitment to others comes an equally heartfelt need to know them on a deep, personal level.

2. Golden retrievers have a strong need for close relationships.

We've mentioned that otters and golden retrievers have natural strengths at building relationships. A big difference between the two, however, is the depth of relationships they enjoy.

Otters make friends easily with all types of people, often knowing a hundred different folks, but only about an inch deep. The goal isn't one incredibly close friendship but many not-so-deep ones. In fact, the average otter can easily have as many as ten to twelve "best" friends—a best friend in the neighborhood, a best friend from school, a best friend from work, a best friend at church, a best friend at the children's school, and so on.

Golden retrievers look at friendships through a

different lens. They usually don't know nearly as many people. But with those they do count as friends, they want to go deep.

That's especially true in a marriage, where the average golden retriever expects the greatest depth of feeling and sharing. Thus, a lion's busyness with projects, a beaver's emotional reserve, or an otter's outgoing personality can become frustrating to the retriever spouse.

Both of our wives have strong golden retriever tendencies, and both of them tend to make friendships for life. Cindy still meets during the Christmas season with ten of her grade-school friends. I (John) can't even remember my grade-school *teachers,* much less ten of my classmates!

Norma has that same retriever depth of friendship. She recently celebrated a special birthday, and the kids and I (Gary) worked for months to put together a successful surprise party.

After Norma walked in the door to a chorus of "Surprise!" and "Happy Birthday!" we seated her in a chair in the living room. Unbeknownst to her, upstairs were several very special friends and relatives waiting to talk to her.

We have an intercom system throughout the house, but on this day it would carry voices from long ago, not music. Like the old television program "This Is Your Life," we'd have one person after another speak into the intercom upstairs and tell some personal story from Norma's past.

Norma could hear the voice, but she couldn't see the person. And each of them would close the story or comment with the words "Do you know who I am?"

Typical otters would be grasping for straws and hoping their natural sense of humor would cover their mistakes. But Norma's recall was perfect. She knew every voice long before the story was finished, and she called each one by name to come down. She didn't even stumble over the voices of three special friends who had been her high-school pals and whom she hadn't seen in many years.

For otters, having the same friends for three weeks is often an accomplishment. They enjoy moving from group to group and focus so much on the future that they don't usually look back. But golden retrievers' deep sense of commitment motivates them to latch on to their loved ones and do all they can to keep them close over the years.

Retrievers are naturally loyal and want deep, lasting friendships. And a third tendency they share is an instinctive expression of their lasting commitment to others.

3. Golden retrievers have a deep need to please others.

We had just finished teaching a section of our "Love Is a Decision" seminar on the various animal personalities when a young mother came up, nearly in tears. "Thank you for what you explained," she said with obvious emotion.

"I finally feel I can relax now. You see, our first child is exactly the way you described the golden retriever. He's loving, sensitive, longs to please us, and hasn't been a problem since I carried him in the womb. But when his brother, the lion, came along . . . It's been war ever since! Now I know why they're so different."

Many parents of golden retrievers share the same experience. They can see in their children a deep desire to please them and others—not in a people-pleasing fashion, as some otters do, but out of genuine best wishes for those to whom they're committed.

A classic example of someone who displays this golden retriever characteristic is Terry Brown, our national seminar coordinator. Terry had been the head of an extremely effective college discipleship program before coming on staff. And when he did come on board, it was with only one goal in mind: to do whatever was needed to serve our ministry and help strengthen families across the country.

For almost six years, Terry has truly been the unsung hero of our ministry. Of the nearly thirty-three thousand people who will attend our "Love Is a Decision" seminar this year, very few will recognize his name. Yet all of them are attending as a direct result of Terry's tireless efforts to set up the host churches, arrange the seminars themselves, get out the information about the seminars, and manage the hundreds of details necessary to the success of such a ministry.[2]

If you have a golden retriever friend like Terry, you're as blessed as we are. Their uncommon willingness to set aside their own needs to serve others is a great virtue.

4. Golden retrievers have hearts full of compassion.

I (Gary) am currently involved in an accountability group of couples that meets every Wednesday. For an hour and a half, we go around the room and share the struggles and successes we've seen since the last meeting.

As a way of breaking down the barriers when we started the group, I had everyone take the Personal Strengths Survey you took earlier. And Shirley, a woman in the group, is a purebred golden retriever if ever there was one. How do I know that? Not just from her test score, but also from hearing what happened recently as she stood in a grocery store line.

Shirley suffers from the same syndrome I do. Namely, whatever line we get in at the bank or grocery store ends up being the slowest one. She was just getting a few things that day, so her junior high son had opted to stay in the car and listen to the radio.

As she patiently stood in line, Shirley smiled at the woman behind her. Perhaps it's the natural warmth that seems to come from golden retrievers or some way the sun reflects off their listening ears, but God seems to have put a clear mark on golden retrievers that lets others know they're His special counselors. And people who are emotionally hurting will spot that mark and start talking—even while standing in a grocery line.

The woman behind Shirley took her cue from the smile and began pouring out her heart. This complete stranger said her husband had left her recently after she had begged him to stay. He was verbally abusive to her and her children, yet she still wanted him back.

On and on went the story of her deep hurts, from her crumbling marriage to losing her job to her young son's catching the flu, which was what had brought her to the store for medicine. Anything that could have gone wrong in this woman's life seemed to have gone wrong.

Finally it was Shirley's turn at the checkout stand, but before she left, she got the woman's name and promised to pray for her. With her bag of groceries, she walked out to the car, put the sack in the back seat, and sat down behind the wheel.

"What took you so long?" her son asked innocently.

Sensitive Shirley looked over at him and burst into tears.

Her son was stunned by her emotion. "Mom, what happened in there?" he asked.

Between sobs, she retold the lady's story, using up two tissues in the process. When she finally finished and dried her eyes, her son shook his head and said, "Mom, *get real.*"

Not all golden retrievers are so sensitive that they wear their tears on their sleeves, but they all feel the hurts of others in their hearts. God has given them an incredible sensitivity.

A good friend told us a classic golden retriever story. Juli is a warm, attractive person who has one of the kindest hearts we've ever seen, and it's not surprising that people take advantage of her listening ear. Several years ago, she sat and listened to a neighbor pour out her sad tale of having to make a sudden move from her home state of Iowa to Arizona, and with a husband who didn't love her. Of all the things she'd had to leave behind, she missed her piano the most.

As Juli's neighbor explained how much that piano meant to her, Juli was deeply touched, and an idea sprang to her mind. She wasn't using the piano she had . . . Why not let this poor, hurting neighbor borrow it? Perhaps by making music she could melt away some of the troubles she faced.

Juli not only loaned her the piano, but she even helped the woman push it down the sidewalk to her house! The small sacrifice of not having her piano for a few weeks wouldn't hurt too much. But she hoped it would help her neighbor a great deal.

Several weeks went by, and Juli didn't hear anything more from her friend. So Juli decided it was time she checked in with her, and she walked down the street to the woman's house—or what *used* to be her home.

In the short time since Juli loaned her piano, the woman's husband had divorced her, and she had moved back to Iowa! With her went the piano Juli's father had given her for her thirteenth birthday!

(She finally got her piano back, but with a broken leg.)

Most golden retrievers won't give you the piano out of their house, but they'll certainly give you the shirt off their back.

Over the years, I (Gary) have learned to accept it as gospel fact whenever Norma says to me, "Uh, oh. Greggie's really hurting" or "Oh, no. I can see Kari had a rough day at school." I might have just seen Greg or Kari, and they looked great to me! But sure enough, my golden retriever wife is so sensitive that she can spot the hurt lying just beneath the surface of our children's lives.

We should note right here that this sensitivity cuts two ways. *The same compassionate heart that can spot the hurts of others can be easily hurt by others as well.*

If you have golden retriever children, they'll be so supportive that they'll mother you if you let them. But don't let them take the full weight of the family's problems on their shoulders.

A loving way to live with golden retrievers is not to wrap them in cotton, but to recognize that they can be more easily hurt than some personalities. Words that may be an emotional pebble to a lion can be a ten-pound weight to a golden retriever's spirit. Respecting their deep capacity for caring and for being hurt themselves is one way to honor them.

The same compassionate heart that can
spot the hurts of others can be easily hurt
by others as well.

Loyalty, deep relationships, a strong desire to please others, and a deep inner sensitivity. That's a strong list of softside character qualities. But the list goes on for this valuable member of the family zoo.

5. Golden retrievers define the word *adaptable*.

Dan was as near the top of the lion scale as you can get, and in a classic marriage of opposites attracting, he married Dana, a purebred golden retriever.

Over the years, Dana became an expert at adaptability. Repeatedly, Dan would walk in the door and announce, "All right, listen up. We're going to the cabin for the weekend, and we're leaving right now!" While all the children would cheer, Dana had to scramble to pack everything they'd need for an unplanned weekend outing.

There were also many times when Dan had a day off from his construction job or was between jobs for a week or more. Often when that happened, Dana would come home from her job and find he'd gotten bored again and gone to work on their house.

She'd walk in and find a wall blown out of one of the bedrooms to add a closet, or the kitchen in the midst of being remodeled. "Oh, Dan," she'd say as she suddenly had to adjust to living for weeks with a construction project underway.

And always she needed to flex around her husband's schedule when he went on summer hours. With the sweltering Texas heat, Dan would head off to the construction site at four o'clock in the morning and expect to be in bed at four o'clock in the afternoon. That meant breakfast had to be started at 3:30 A.M. and the kids kept quiet in the afternoon while he slept.

Being adaptable was a strength that helped Dana keep some kind of harmony at home. But we know that for some people, this positive golden retriever quality can become a terrible weakness.

In the chapters upcoming on developing hardside love, we'll mention a concept getting considerable attention these days called codependency.[3] In short, this term refers to someone who is an enabler, but not in the normally positive sense. These enablers are like the wife who "protects" her alcoholic husband by lying to his boss about why he's missed work; or the son who enables his mother to continue her tyrannical domination of his own wife and family by never being willing to confront her in strength.

If you're a golden retriever who has seen your strength of adaptability become pushed to an extreme, you've got the potential for a very serious and painful problem. That's why we strongly encourage you to read on and learn how to give *both* sides of love to the people in your home.

Thus far, we've seen five characteristics of golden retrievers. But they have two other traits that sound like exceptions to the rule of loving softness. The first we'll look at is that while they are indeed very adaptable on the outside, it comes at a high cost on the inside.

6. Golden retrievers often react to sudden changes.

If you have someone with strong retriever traits in your home, let us tell you four words that can help strengthen your relationship like almost nothing else. The four words are: Prepare them for change.

Lions and otters thrive on change. They can't wait to change something, even if it's for no other reason than just to put their mark on something. That's why these individuals have such a problem ordering from a menu. They want to be able to substitute a substitute for their substitute. And it drives beaver waitresses crazy!

Lions and otters don't just change menu selection, however. They're fully capable of making major changes without any warning—like coming home and saying, "Guess where we're moving, Honey?" or "Guess what job I took today?" And when they do this to the people they tend most often to marry—golden retrievers—at times they see something unexpected: their spouse's teeth bared in a snarl.

It hurts golden retrievers' feelings and their deep sense of fairness to be left out of a decision. It also makes them feel as if they're being used when they have to go along with something they had no part in discussing. Normally, they'll still fall in step out of their strong sense of loyalty, but they pay a high emotional price to do it.

A few pages back, we mentioned how thankful we are for Terry Brown, our ministry partner. Each month, Terry has to travel to our seminar site with two off-the-chart otters: us. And each month, he deserves a medal for putting up with our natural tendency to change things.

Several months ago, Terry finally reached his saturation point. He had put up with the way we talk every waitress into making a special order of everything—even toast. He hadn't complained when we changed rental car companies the minute we flew into a city, even though he had taken the time to reserve a car. He actually didn't mind too much our habit of changing hotels the way other people change socks. But we finally brought him to the end of his rope one day when we walked into the seminar room an hour before the program started and began to switch the location and arrangement of the book table.

For us, it was just the fun of having something else to change. But for Terry, who had spent hours figuring out the best place and the best way to display items and then setting up, it became a personal affront. We didn't see the problem—that is, until we closed his spirit so tightly that it became obvious we all needed to have a long talk.

Terry had done his best to put up with all the sudden changes, but our love of rearranging everything was actually very dishonoring to him. When we finally realized the negative message that changing the book table an hour before the seminar was sending him, we backed off and asked his forgiveness.

Those four words, "Prepare them for change," took on the form of a goal for us, and it led us to make some very real changes. Now if you were to travel with us to a seminar city, you'd see that we don't switch rental cars on Terry without letting him know well in advance. We've also learned to say, "Here's an idea to change the whole structure of the seminar—but not for a year or so. What do you think about it, Terry?" And we've learned to stay in the same hotel for more than one night.

Have we stopped using a menu as a starting point for negotiations? Well, we're not perfect! But at least Terry knows we're *trying* to honor him by preparing him before we change things, and that has gone a long way toward cementing our already strong relationships.

Do you have a golden retriever son or daughter who needs extra time to think about a major family decision or move? Do you have a spouse who doesn't need to hear, "Guess where we're going tonight?" but "Honey, I'd like us to go out tomorrow night. What do you think?"

Golden retrievers, of all the animals in the family zoo, are often the easiest to take advantage of. Their ability to love others deeply is what makes them vulnerable to someone who would exploit their softside strengths. But that's not to say they're emotional marshmallows.

7. Golden retrievers hold stubbornly to what they feel is right.

Don't draw the conclusion from what we've said that golden retrievers are wimps. They certainly are softer in attitude and action than the average lion, but many of them still possess incredible courage and strength.

Take a man from the Tennessee mountains named Alvin York, who reached manhood as World War I raged in Europe. In a dramatic way, after he was struck by lightning, he came to know Christ personally. As a result, he made a total about-face from his wild and rebellious ways to a solid commitment to Jesus. But then the war came along, and it reached into the hills of Tennessee and selected this newly transformed golden retriever for the draft.

York was a crack shot. He had won fame in a land of sharpshooters by winning all the local turkey shoots. He had fought and drunk with the worst of them in his non-Christian days, and he had come close to murdering a man who had tricked him in a business deal.

He was no coward. He wasn't any more afraid of going to war than the next man. But he had the Bible to deal with now, and it was the genuine fear of God that gave him pause. There was no denying that there were verses in the Bible that told him it was wrong to kill, and he had to deal with them before he could make a wholehearted commitment to the Army.

Reporting to boot camp, York quickly won the rank of corporal. But he struggled so much with his conscience that his commanding officer sent him back home to spend time in prayer and make up his mind. If he returned and asked for it, he would be granted conscientious-objector status. But if he returned with his inner questions answered, he would join his men who were waiting to be sent overseas.

Golden retrievers will follow all day behind a leader they respect. But try pushing them and they won't budge an inch. York's commanding officer knew his backwoodsman needed time to think instead of a push. And sending this new recruit home turned out to be the wisest thing he ever did.

Alvin York returned from Tennessee convinced in his heart and mind that he should join in his country's fight. And armed with that conviction, there was no stopping him. In fact, on October 8, 1918, in the trenches of France, he did something nearly unheard of in modern warfare.

York had been ordered to take a small patrol and reconnoiter a line of German machine gun nests. The enemy spotted their advance, however, and poured down small arms and machine gun fire, effectively trapping him and his men. Ignoring his personal safety, York crawled under fire to a flanking position and began firing round after round into the enemy troops.

With his expert marksmanship, he killed twenty-five Germans as he advanced down the trenches from machine gun nest to machine gun nest. Finally, in desperation, the next group of German soldiers threw up their hands.

A major was in the group he captured, and York then forced him to order all his men to surrender. With nearly thirty prisoners in hand, York began walking back to the Allied lines.

Along the way, other German soldiers saw the troops being marched under guard by the lone American. The sight of one man leading so many troops made them think their entire line had collapsed, and they, too, began surrendering to Corporal York in droves.

When this mountain man from Tennessee finally reached the American field headquarters, he had 132 prisoners in tow! And along the way, he had recruited only 3 other soldiers to bring them all in.

Corporal Alvin C. York was promoted to Sergeant Alvin C. York, and he also received the Congressional Medal of Honor for his bravery that day. French General Ferdinand Foch said of York, "The gallantry and courage exhibited by Corporal York was unsurpassed by any private soldier of all the armies of Europe."[4]

If you'd like to relive his incredible story and learn more about the stubborn strength of a golden retriever, we highly recommend you rent *Sergeant York*, a movie on videotape starring Gary Cooper in the title role. Cooper gives an Academy-Award-winning portrayal of a genuine Christian hero. It's one of the few movies Hollywood has produced that's well worth watching. (Another, telling the story of golden retriever Eric Liddell, is *Chariots of Fire.*)

Golden retrievers can hold as strongly to what they believe is right as anyone alive. And they're often the ones putting their very lives on the line to back up their convictions.

We've seen seven sterling qualities that capture some of what golden retrievers convey to others. Each makes them a valuable part of a friendship, family or work situation. Once again, those traits are:

1. Golden retrievers are loyal.
2. Golden retrievers have a strong need for close relationships.
3. Golden retrievers have a deep need to please others.
4. Golden retrievers have hearts full of compassion.
5. Golden retrievers define the word *adaptable*.
6. Golden retrievers often react to sudden changes.
7. Golden retrievers hold stubbornly to what they feel is right.

The Perfect Example

At this point, we've looked at all four animals in the family zoo and seen that they fall into pairs when it comes to leaning toward hardside or softside love. Lions and beavers tend to be hard on problems, but they're often hard on people as well. And otters and golden retrievers tend to be soft on people, but too often they're also soft on problems they face.

Is there any way to take the best of each of these personalities and blend it into one person? There *is* for those who seek to pattern their lives after the Savior's.

Jesus Christ had all the strengths of a lion. He was decisive and a leader. As the Lion of Judah, He faced up to even the hardest of trials. But He was also a beaver; doing things right, by the book, and in a quality way that resulted in works and words that will stand forever.

Further, Jesus carried the strengths of an otter. He loved celebrations (the first place He took the disciples was to a wedding) and motivating others to godliness, and He was comfortable with crowds and initiating contact with people He had never met. Yet He was also a golden retriever; always going deeper than surface level with His disciples and followers, faithful to keep His promises, and loyal all the way to the cross.

But is a balanced life that reflects both sides of love reserved only for Christ? What about those of us with clay feet?

In the four chapters that follow, you'll discover twenty ways to help you become more balanced in your love for others. First, we'll look at ten ways in which hardside people can add softness to their lives. Then we'll tackle an even harder task: we'll examine ten ways in which softside people can add a healthy hardness to their love.

We can't be Jesus. But we're called to be like Him. *And it's in discovering how to love others the way He did that we can grow even closer to Him and our loved ones.*

Are you ready to see your love for others grow deeper and stronger than ever before? That can happen as you turn the page and discover a number of practical ways to increase commitment, affection and closeness.

8

Increasing Softside Love, Part I

Few things do more damage to a home than having one member be far out of balance. And we're astounded at the way one hardside event has the power to weaken instantly the bonds holding a family together. That fact was brought home to me (Gary) dramatically several years ago.

It was the summer of 1982, and Norma and I had packed up our kids, tents and swim wear and headed out to one of the many lakes in the Chicago area. Some friends from our church, Charles and Pat, had accompanied us with their three children, who were close to the same ages as our own.

We pitched our tents on a grassy rise overlooking

a narrow, sandy beach, just yards from the lake. After breakfast that first morning, Greg and Mike matched up with our friends' boys and trooped off to explore the shoreline. That left the rest of us to clean the dishes and set out what we'd need for lunch.

After straightening up the campsite, we all went down to the beach to sunbathe and swim. The air was already warm and muggy as I waded into the surprisingly cold water, preparing to do some snorkeling.

I remember looking over at our families on the beach as I adjusted my mask. Nothing could have appeared more relaxed and peaceful. Charles and his wife and daughter were spreading out their blankets on the sand. And right beside them, Norma and my Kari were already settled down, putting on suntan lotion.

With all the world seemingly at peace, I took a deep breath and plunged underwater. After staying down as long as I could, I came back to the surface, blew the water out of my snorkel, and swam in a lazy circle for a few minutes. I watched the water get deeper as I moved away from shore, and I enjoyed looking down at the waving, green seaweed and few small fish that darted underneath me.

When I had completed the circle and come back to shallow water, I stood up, pushed up my mask, and wiped the water from my eyes. That's when I looked back to shore and saw a far different scene from the one of just a few minutes before.

Everything had looked like a Norman Rockwell

picture when I submerged: calm, peaceful, relaxed. Now it looked like a nightmare scene that Stephen King would have scripted.

Charles and his ten-year-old daughter stood at the edge of the sand, screaming at each other. Then the scene got far worse. At the height of the shouting match, when his daughter refused to do something he asked, Charles slapped her with the back of his hand, sending her flying backward into the water.

Charles's wife and Norma immediately became hysterical, screaming at him and running to help his daughter. In an instant, an angry, hardside father had shattered everyone's relaxing weekend —but even more so his relationship with his daughter.

The Dark Side of Hardside Love

At the time of that incident, I hadn't met anyone who was harder on people, especially his family, than my friend Charles. But what happened that terrible morning became one of the keys that forced Charles to add softness to his life. As a result of the confrontation that followed, Charles not only apologized to everyone, but he also finally took the much-needed step of going into counseling.

For several years, he spent time in small support groups, dealing with his own background, which included parents who deserted him and major incidents of abuse with a step-family. It took time, tears of shame and a painful confrontation with the truth, but he finally saw his present anger as his own problem, not something he could explain away or blame on his parents or past.

Through the painful process of facing the truth, Charles did begin to change. In fact, he changed so much that he has learned to communicate even the hardest things to his daughter with the soft side of love.

Even the Hardest Can Learn

That day at the lake, Charles had struck his daughter for talking back to him and not taking his advice. Seven years later, he sat down with her to discuss something that was potentially just as explosive.

At age seventeen, like most young ladies, his daughter was looking forward to dating. One boy at school had been talking with her at length and was interested in taking her out. However, not only was he a non-Christian, but he had also earned the reputation of being one of the wildest boys in the school.

In times past, Charles would have put his foot down if his daughter had even brought up the subject of dating such a boy. But he had learned much over the previous seven years. He had discovered that having only one side of love isn't enough to sustain a relationship, much less cause it to grow. What's more, he knew there was far greater power to change others through adding softness to his love than in all his angry lectures combined.

With that insight, Charles took his daughter out on a date night (now a regular occurrence between the two of them). Over dinner, he did something that again brought tears to her eyes, but this time for a different reason. At this meeting, instead of angry words, he used a softsided word picture to communicate his concern. (As we point out in our book *The Language of Love*, emotional word pictures are the best tool we know to carry hard or soft words right to a person's heart.)

Charles told her that she was like a precious diamond to him. And as they would do with a priceless gem, he and her mother were trying to keep her protected until her wedding day. He went on to tell her that he prayed each day that she would find the right kind of boys to date: young men who would realize what a treasure she was and wouldn't do anything to deface that priceless diamond.

He made sure she knew he didn't object to her dating. He pulled out the list of character traits they had all agreed should be a consistent part of her life before she began dating. Then he went on to tell her how she possessed each one and was certainly free to go out.

What concerned him wasn't her readiness but the character of this boy who was asking her out. To let her date him would be like handing over his precious treasure to someone who would put it on the concrete sidewalk and then use a sledgehammer to mar it.

By the end of his story, she was so moved by the picture of her father's love and saw so clearly his reason for saying no that she didn't even argue. She agreed this young man wasn't the kind of person she wanted to date, and she ended up having a meaningful talk with him about the Lord!

Charles is still a perfectionist and a consistent disciplinarian. He's still hard on problems. But to his natural hard side he has learned to add the other side of love with his daughter and others. He can now make his point without raising his voice or shaking his finger.

The Secret of Being Soft

Even for people as hard as Charles, it's never too late to learn the secret of being soft. You don't have to be born with a soft spirit to learn to display one.

As we pointed out in chapter 2, neither of us is tender by nature. But we've learned to work at it. And in developing our own soft sides, as well as in counseling with others, we've found there are ten methods that, if put into practice, can help people add Christlike softness to their lives. Together, these methods can begin to take the cutting edge off hard personalities and draw us closer to others than ever before.

If you scored high on the beaver or lion scale, you'll find the next two chapters particularly helpful. The intensity and drive that most lions show, and the emotional reserve and desire to do things by the book that most beavers share, are indeed strengths. To the other animals in the family zoo, however, they can often project a hardside distance.

That's why it's so important to understand what balances the two sides of love if we're to see our affection for others really communicated. With that in mind, to add healthy softness to our lives, we must learn to do the following things.

1. Deal with emotional "freeze points" in the past.

Time and again in counseling, we've seen that something from a person's past is contributing greatly to out-of-balance relationships in the present. When we get to the heart of the person's problems, we find the free flow of balanced love blocked by what we call an emotional freeze point.

Emotional freeze points reflect either a
single event or a season of events that lock a
person into giving only one side of love.

Emotional freeze points reflect either a single event or a season of events that lock a person into giving only one side of love. Consider what happened to Barbara.

Her father, Jim, sat at his desk at work one day. It was already late, time to be heading home. But that wasn't on Jim's mind this day. Instead, his hand shook slightly as he picked up the phone.

The call lasted less than two minutes. All it took was dialing seven numbers, issuing a few well-thought-out words, and bingo, he had accomplished what he wanted. As he hung up, he sighed in relief and then reached for his coat.

In his mind, he had simply closed the book on a bad story he had been living for too long. But at the other end of the line, it was as if a time bomb had just gone off . . .

Barbara was beginning to set up for the anniversary party later that night. She dragged the nice silverware from under the tablecloths in the china cabinet and began polishing the pieces at the dining room table. With her hands occupied, she let her mind flip back to the many pictures pasted in her memory.

Barb's father had never been physically abusive to her. But in some ways, his critical, hurtful words had hit just as hard as any blows he could have landed.

Barb shook her head to clear her mind of all the negative pictures and emotions that had flooded her thoughts. This wasn't the sort of day to be dragging up difficult memories. For all their problems, her mother and father had still endured twenty-five years together.

It was their anniversary! Soon a few friends and family members would be coming over for a small but carefully planned dinner party. As she finished putting up the last of the streamers, she had to smile. *If nothing else,* she thought, *at least they've stayed together.*

That one positive fact had always been an encouragement to her. Their willingness to stay married had acted like an anchor to help her ride out the emotional storms she saw blowing daily in their marriage. Little did she know that the fragile cable holding their commitment was about to snap.

It wasn't unusual for Barb's father to call from work and say he was running late. In fact, with guests set to arrive at any moment, she knew it was probably him calling as her mother walked over to pick up the phone. What she didn't know was that this call didn't come spontaneously as her father looked up at the shop clock. He had been planning for months what he was going to say and when he would call.

Barb couldn't hear the conversation taking place in the next room, but it was soon clear that a tragedy was taking place. After a few moments of stunned silence and interrupted sentences, her mother finally gasped and slumped into a chair near the phone. Tears streamed from her eyes.

"What's wrong, Mother? What happened?" Barb cried, running across the hall to her side. When she got no response, she said still louder, "Tell me what's wrong!"

Grabbing the phone that now hung limp in her mother's hand she shouted into the receiver, "Who is this? What's going on?" The only answer she got was an impersonal, irritating dial tone.

"Mother," she said, grabbing her by the arms, "what happened?"

"It's your father," Barb's mom said in a voice

just above a whisper. "He's not going to be at the party. He's not coming home—not ever."

"Why, Mother?" she asked, trying to make some sense out of what had happened.

"He's leaving me for another woman," she said, her face the picture of shock. "And he wanted to wait until today to tell me."

Never once in eighteen years had Barbara seen her mother lose her temper. But that night, as she got up from the chair and walked toward her bedroom, Barb's mother stopped at the dining room table, gaily decorated for the festivities.

With a fierce swing, she sent flying the beautiful centerpiece, a large, crystal vase filled with water and twenty-five long-stem roses. Shocked with herself and overcome by emotion, she ran crying into the bedroom, slamming the door behind her.

A shattered vase was the perfect picture of Barbara's world. Each time the doorbell rang that night, she had to relive and retell the heartache of her father's call to a confused, concerned guest. And each day thereafter, her heart was broken in pieces as she watched her mother go through an unwanted, ugly divorce.

End of the story? We wish it were. But one final tragedy slammed home a message to us like an iron fist.

As Barbara told us about what her father had done, she was looking back in time. Instead of being eighteen, she was now thirty-four, married and with a promising career.

At a Christian businesswomen's meeting where I (John) was teaching the concepts found in this book, Barbara came up afterward with tears in her eyes. "As you've been talking, I realized something important," she said. "The very night my father called home and said he was leaving, I made a major decision. I was looking into my mother's bedroom, watching her cry and seeing her whole world fall apart.

"That's when I said to myself, *I will never, ever, let anyone treat me like my father has treated my mother.* But what I was really saying was that *I would never be soft like my mother.* I would never let anyone get close to me and hurt me the way she was hurt."

Tragically, Barbara's decision to totally block the soft side of love was carried out with frightening efficiency. In tears she told me, "Now, after eight years of marriage, my husband just left me! After your talk, I know why. He's told me a hundred times. It's because I'm too hard with him. But after what happened with my mother, I could never be soft with him or anyone I love."

That's just one story out of a hundred we could have related about a traumatic memory in a child's life that locked that person into loving others halfheartedly. We've seen emotional freeze points caused by a divorce, death in the family, physical abuse, a difficult move, failing to get into a particular profession, or some other single situation that blocked off one side of love.

But emotional freeze points can't always be traced back to a single event. In Charles's situation (at the beginning of this chapter), it was a season of tragedies that froze his ability to give the soft side of love.

Charles's mother had dropped him and his brother off at an orphanage when he was five because she "just couldn't handle the stress" of raising them anymore. Both at the orphanage and in several difficult foster homes, he went through more instances of abuse than he wanted to remember. His mother's absence and each new incidence of abuse left unresolved anger in his life, freezing his heart harder and harder, blocking his ability to give or receive softside love.

If you struggle with giving others one side of love, especially its soft side, begin by taking two steps back and looking closely at your past. And as a way to help you do this, ask yourself questions like these:

Did you see a balance of softside and hardside love in your home? If not, toward what extreme was it shifted?

Are you aware of a specific situation or season in your parents' past that may have blocked them from giving you both sides of love?

Do you see yourself giving the same sides of love to your children that you received from your parents? Does that please or concern you?

Can you think of a specific time when you made an inner decision that you were not going to be soft or hard with others? What prompted the decision?

How was God pictured in your childhood home? Did you receive a balanced view of Him, or was He only a softside God of mercy or a hardside God of judgment? How has this past view of God affected your view of Him today?

Perhaps already, like Charles and Barbara, you can identify a situation or season that caused you to make an internal decision blocking one side of love. If you sense such a blockage in your life, you need to do a little digging in your background.

Honestly facing the past is the beginning of thawing out from an emotional freeze point. If your struggle to love others wholeheartedly today comes out of a reaction to your past, a number of resources can help you in going deeper and gaining freedom. Take the time to look up some of these helps in the Notes section at the back of the book.[1] In addition, you can apply the remaining nine ways to add softness to your life.

2. Recognize that certain personality bents can set up barriers to softside love.

One of the strongest desires we hear from women across the country is for closeness in marriage.

They long for an intimate connection with their spouses, especially when it comes to sharing their feelings, needs, hurts and desires. Yet there can be a natural barrier to softside love growing out of the different ways the four basic personalities view distance and closeness.

Lions and beavers (and especially those who score high in both scales) share certain characteristics. For example, they both like to accomplish things and make sure they're done right. And in many cases; they're also more comfortable with distance than with closeness. What do we mean by that?

Lions lean toward distance in relationships for several reasons. For some, the tendency comes from a deep dislike, even fear, of being controlled. Lions want to be in charge. They also know that the more they share of themselves or give others a say in situations, the less they determine the outcome of a conversation or decision.

Keeping themselves at a distance gives them a great deal of power in a relationship. One reason this is true is that the person who acts the least connected usually holds the most power cards. Think back to junior high for a picture of what we mean.

Remember the girl who was five inches taller than most boys in seventh grade but who stole their hearts anyway? Perhaps it was her perfume or her turned-up nose. But whatever the reason, the harder it was to win her attention, the more the boys tried to gain it. As long as she was cool toward their advances, they were kept on their toes. Her staying a distance from them kept them trying to please her by spending all their allowance on cards and presents she didn't really like.

If you add lions' desire for power, their natural inner intensity, and a lack of fear of confrontation, it's easy to see how they can look so strong and majestic. But for loved ones wanting to get close to them, they can appear to be isolated in their own fenced-in land, far from any personal encounters.

In short, lions are often comfortable with emotional distance because it gives them power in dealing with others. Unfortunately, this distance can sometimes feel like an uncrossable emotional gulf for those who want a close relationship.

Beavers, too, can communicate a high degree of emotional distance, which in turn can convey a lack of emotional attachment and warmth. However, the breathing room they seek from others ties in with their reflective nature and deep desire to do things right.

Their critical bent is an unquestioned strength. However, if their critical skills are pushed out of balance, they can easily put people on the spot with their questions, causing them to draw back. Even more, their caution and emotional reserve can be like wearing a sign that says, "I'm too busy to talk with you now" or "I need space, so don't come any closer."

Even more than lions, beavers are comfortable

with distance in a relationship. A woman named Sandy told us recently that after more than twenty years of marriage, she was ready to throw in the towel. She and her husband, Phil, had settled into a daily pattern of speaking ten words or less to each other. She longed not only for more conversation, but for more of him as well.

Talking to Phil revealed that there wasn't another woman, nor did he have an all-consuming job. He was simply an extreme beaver who *enjoyed* the distance between them. He liked being around her, but not being close to her. And he also liked the long periods of silence and felt threatened when she made efforts to draw closer.

We all need some degree of distance from others. But out-of-balance beavers can communicate, even unintentionally, an aloofness, a lack of need for others and a rigidity that nonverbally pushes people away.

Whom do hardsided lions and beavers tend to marry or have as children, however? That's right, softsided otters and golden retrievers. *And otters and golden retrievers have as strong a natural desire to move closer to others as lions and beavers do to move away.*

Otters can quickly share their hearts with people, even those they don't know well. Some otters are capable of making friends with strangers on an elevator if the ride is longer than three floors. And golden retrievers have an even greater need for a close connection with others. As far as they're concerned, no relationship is successful if it doesn't go any deeper than the surface.

What this means in many homes is that the race is on between otters and golden retrievers who are pushing forward, wanting that close connection with their spouses, while lions and beavers see them coming and pull back just as quickly.

What do distance and closeness have to do with developing the soft side of love? If people don't allow others to come close to them both physically and emotionally, they'll almost always fail at trying to communicate softside love.

Otters and golden retrievers have as strong a natural desire to move closer to others as lions and beavers do to move away.

We can't tell you the number of now-grown children who longed for a parent to come closer. Nearly each week in counseling, we see a spouse who has tried for years to draw the other person into the relationship and been pushed back each time.

There is a way, however, to stop this distance/closeness dance, shrinking the gap between people and helping them gain the closeness they need for a strong relationship. It begins by first gaining a clear picture of the current distance or closeness between you and others.

Take a moment to answer the questions below. They'll help you to see how close or far away you are from others. Then share the results with your spouse.

Smalley/Trent Distance-Closeness Survey

Answer the following questions with particular loved ones in mind (e.g., your mate, child, close friend, parent). Fill in the blank with a number between 1 and 4, indicating your answer to each question as follows:

$$1 = \text{never} \qquad 3 = \text{often}$$
$$2 = \text{seldom} \qquad 4 = \text{always}$$

With your loved ones, do you . . .

- Give them the freedom to ask you questions without reacting or becoming defensive? _____

- Seek to hear their real inner feelings without ridiculing them? _____
- Freely express your own inner feelings and thoughts? _____
- Know clearly their ideas and plans for the future? _____
- Watch your everyday manners so as not to offend them? _____
- Plan your schedule to include time with them? _____

- "Light up" when they return from a trip? _____

- Say "I love you" regularly and without conditions? _____
- Share your personal problems and victories? _____
- Laugh regularly? _____

- Actively attend or support their hobbies or athletic events? _____
- Regularly hug or kiss them? _____
- Seek and value their opinions on family issues first? _____
- Pray with and for them regularly? _____
- Keep yourself well-dressed and manicured? _____
- Build their trust by being consistently honest with them? _____
- Actively listen to them by putting down the paper, turning off the television, or looking up from cooking? _____
- Allow them to borrow your things? _____
- Smile toward them regularly? _____
- Seek their forgiveness immediately when you've offended them? _____
- Attend church together regularly? _____
- Keep their secrets if they want you to? _____
- Keep your promises? _____
- Show an honest interest in their friends and relatives? _____
- Act cheerful and encouraging? _____
- Make a genuine effort to be on time? _____
- Watch your tone of voice? _____
- Do your fair share of the housework? _____
- Respect their personal property? _____
- Avoid using negative nicknames? _____

The highest score you can get on this survey is 120; the lowest, 30. If you're in the top third of the range (90-120), you can be fairly certain your loved ones are sensing your attachment and closeness. If you're somewhat in the middle, you may need to ask how connected your loved ones feel to you. However, our counseling experience indicates that if you scored at the bottom end of the distance scale (45 or less), *your independence from others is probably being perceived by them as unhealthy distance.*

Please understand that it's important to have a healthy degree of emotional distance. Some families are so close that if one member sneezes, everyone else reaches for a tissue. People need enough independence that they're able to stand on their own feet. But in marriage and as parents we need to be close enough physically and emotionally to communicate warmth and love.

What's the answer to a distance problem in our relationships? Is it just to say, "That's the way I am! I'm not naturally a close person. My parents weren't close. My grandparents weren't close. My great-grandparents weren't close"?

Not if we're serious about giving others the two sides of love they need so much—or about reflecting God's kind of love.

We know it can be difficult to give up the protective comfort of emotional distance. It can be scary to get close to someone, particularly if we've been hurt in the past. But keeping others at more than arm's length can easily turn into a selfish distance that allows us to go our own way without making the kind of significant attachments for which our family members and close friends long.

If you've found yourself with far more distance

than closeness in your family or friendships, increasing your softside skills can help you bridge the gap. And one of those skills is our third step toward building softness into your life.

3. Learn to give others a "softness sandwich."

My (Gary's) youngest son's football coach is one of the best in the area. But he became an even better coach this past year by learning to give his players what we call a "softness sandwich."

Jack, our coach, is a former professional football player. And like many coaches, he has a great deal of lion in him. That's understandable. There's nothing soft about taking a team through the rigors of two-a-day practices or making players run windsprints in Arizona in August to get them in shape for the season. What Jack has realized, however, is that hardness alone won't motivate every player on the team.

In Jack's first year here, he was really frustrated by his inability to motivate a number of players. Some of his top prospects even quit the team, leaving him with glaring holes in his lineup. Interestingly, the kids he was having trouble with were almost all golden retriever personalities.

After practice one day, he expressed his frustration to me. "I know I'm tough with these boys," he said emphatically. "But they've got to get motivated and intense. They need to get with it, or maybe they need to bag football and go out for some other sport."

"Coach," I said, "are you open to a suggestion?"

"Our season starts in three weeks," he said. "At this point, I'm willing to listen to anything."

That's when I gave him a two-minute explanation of the different animal personalities and told him about the softness sandwich that John and I teach in counseling.

"Coach, try an experiment for one week of practice," I said. "For every thirty seconds you spend getting on a player about a missed tackle or assignment, leave him with thirty seconds of softness as well. Look him right in the eye and tell him what he did wrong and how it might cost the team in a real game. But then put your arm around him, tell him you appreciate him, and tell him he's too good a player to make mistakes like that. Then send him back onto the field.

"Remember, thirty seconds of hardness surrounded by thirty seconds of being soft. *But make sure you leave with softness when you can.*"

Jack looked skeptical, and understandably. Most of the coaching done on anything but the most elementary level has become 99 percent hardside. The idea of sandwiching softness in with his hardside lectures obviously made him uncomfortable. But he was willing to try anything.

Old patterns are hard to break. In fact, at the end of the first practice where he tried this approach, he asked me, "Gary, when I talk with them and softly touch them, *can I be holding them around the neck?*"

But Jack did change, and so, dramatically, did the attitudes of many of the "problem" players on the team. He had a softside talk with each of the boys who had left the team, and he won nearly all of them back. He also came within one series and a missed field goal of winning the state football championship outright last year, settling for a tie and the title of co-champion.

Jack is an excellent coach, and adding softness only increased his success. Time and again, we've seen spouses and parents win a loved one's heart back by learning and practicing this same approach. Take Laurie, for example.

Laurie keeps the kind of house germs hate. As a very high beaver, she keeps her home so clean that germs don't even visit anymore. Unfortunately, her otter husband's idea of keeping things clean is straightening out his closet once a year whether it needs it or not.

During their early years of marriage, Laurie's natural hardside bent was pushed far into the critical zone. At least twenty times a day, she would find some reason to criticize her husband's behavior. He had put the bath mat fuzzy side up again, not fuzzy side down. He had taken a shower without wiping off the glass again. He had driven her car, and there were crumbs everywhere from his snack at the mini mart. On and on her list went.

The harder she became with her husband, trying to force him to change, the fewer results she saw. But when she began to practice the softness sandwich approach, she was shocked at the change that took place in him *and* in her.

"I made a decision that I wouldn't criticize Bill

about something he'd done or failed to do unless I could say something positive to him as well," she said. "At first, I found myself not saying anything at all. It was so foreign to me to try to link a positive with a negative. I felt funny and two-faced. But in time, all I can say is that the change in both of us has been remarkable."

Why is softness such a key to decreasing conflict in a home? Studies have shown that the happiest couples are those who consistently do small acts of caring (particularly soft actions like a kind word, a gentle touch or an encouraging note), even during times of expressing concerns.[2] On the other hand, with the most unhealthy and conflictful couples, softside actions are next to nonexistent.

Thus, if we want to have the healthiest possible relationships, we'll learn to include a sandwich of softness with our hardside correction.

We've looked at three important ways of adding softness to our lives: spotting emotional freeze points from our past, recognizing and cutting down on the emotional distance in our homes, and learning how to use a softness sandwich when we need to correct someone. Each of these is important. But there are seven more powerful ways to increase this important side of love.

9

Increasing Softside Love, Part II

We've already seen three keys to communicating love's soft side. A fourth involves looking at softness from the perspective of others.

4. Understand what softness means to the other person.

Varying personalities make it inevitable that people will view a given situation differently. And if a marriage or parent-child relationship is to flourish, we need to value each other's differing personality strengths and learn, in light of them, how best to communicate softness to the other person. *Conversely, the less we appreciate a person's natural strengths, the harder we'll tend to act toward that individual.*

Remember the story of Jessica and her mother that began chapter 3? Jessica was a beaver by temperament and had to do things carefully. Her mother, on the other hand, was a lion who wanted everything done quickly and efficiently. But this wise mother learned to apply a powerful biblical principle that put more softness into her relationship with her daughter than ever before.

In the book of Matthew, Christ told us regarding our spiritual affections, "For where your treasure is, there your heart will be also."[1] What's true in the spiritual realm is also true in our families. The more we learn to treasure our loved ones' natural bents and talents, especially if they're different from our own, the softer our hearts will be toward them.

That's exactly what happened between Jessica and her mother. As this woman grew in her appreciation of Jessica's unique strengths, she wanted to learn what softness meant to her daughter. So she asked simply, "What are some ways in which I can be softer with you?"

Jessica immediately gave an answer that shocked her mother: "You can turn off the timer when I'm doing my homework."

Having to do her homework with the clock ticking in the background wasn't training Jessica to go faster; it was frustrating her into making mistakes and causing her to go even slower.

Jessica's mom liked working under the clock. It

was a natural assumption that her daughter would, too. But God had given Jessica a different perspective on time, and problems began to develop when those two time zones crossed. The gift of unpressured time was one practical way her mother could demonstrate a softer love.

The less we appreciate a person's natural strengths, the harder we'll tend to act toward that individual.

Are you making demands on someone you love that are pushing the person away from you, perhaps hardening your own heart as well? Sometimes softside love comes wrapped up in the consideration to call before you bring a guest home to dinner. Other times it means dealing with procrastination and beginning your taxes before 10:00 P.M. on April 14. It may even mean being sensitive enough to make sure the dirty clothes go *inside* the laundry basket, not just on the floor next to it. And always it means a shoulder to cry on rather than a lecture.

In each case, learning to value others' differences, and especially *asking* what softness means to them, can give you insight into large and small ways to touch their hearts and soften yours.

5. Learn the secret of making hard decisions in a soft way.

All this talk about adding softness seemed like the last thing the Smiths needed to hear. After all, they were in the middle of a power struggle with their twelve-year-old son.

They had tried being soft with him, even to the point of bribing him to bring his behavior into line. But nothing seemed to work with their lion son short of bringing the hammer down in a harsh confrontation. Both mother and father were golden retrievers by nature, however, and having to hammer their son each day was breaking their own hearts.

Contrary to appearances, softness was actually the major thing this home needed. Why?

At the heart of many discipline problems is anger—often the immature anger of a child who wants his or her own way and rebels against any controls or boundaries. Unfortunately, in response to a child's anger, parents frequently decide to meet fire with fire, and the situation can escalate quickly to World War III proportions.

Until children grow to where they can stand shoulder to shoulder with Mom or Dad, parents can normally out-shout them and force them to follow the rules for a short time. But like tossing a bucket of gasoline on a small fire to try to put it out, the cumulative effect of anger in a home can cause even greater long-term damage.

We all know how easy it is to meet anger with anger. But what can turn away anger instead? The Scriptures tell us one thing decreases the presence of this damaging emotion in a home: softness.

Biblical paradoxes like "A gentle answer turns away wrath" and "A gentle tongue can break a bone"[2] are intriguing, but they're not always comforting, especially for a family like the Smiths. How can you add softness to a problem situation without handing over the home to an unruly child? What can help a mom and dad go back to being parents, not full-time police?

The Smiths and many other families need a tool for making hard decisions in a soft way—a method that increases a family's commitment to face a problem, task or goal together while decreasing tension at the same time. We've seen this method work in our own homes and in hundreds of others.

The method to which we refer is the family contract. Let's illustrate this tool with the example of the Murphy family, who faced the same problem many others do. Namely, they have the whole family zoo under one roof.

Ed, the father, is a lion and wants the family to run like a well-oiled machine. His son the otter, Sam, keeps throwing monkey wrenches into the machine. That leaves the mother, Doris, the golden retriever, constantly on call, trying to patch up things between the two men in her household. What about their daughter, Betty the beaver? She uses her critical skills to point out her brother's every fault while being close to perfect herself, starting the fireworks all over again.

Instead of suffering constant pandemonium and family friction, however, they learned to put even the hardest family rules into a soft enough form for everyone to swallow, including Sam—a mutually agreed upon family contract.

One evening, they all took stock of their situation. None of them was happy with the way things were going, but no one wanted to budge to make things better (except golden retriever Mom, of course, who had already bent herself out of shape trying to keep everyone happy).

Ed took charge of the meeting and had them all list what they wanted from their family. Once he had compiled everyone's lists, he boiled down their wants into three primary rules they all needed to live by. While each major category would have subcategories under it, the three rules they agreed to were:

1. Honor God.
2. Honor each other.
3. Honor God's creation.

Honoring God, they felt, meant regular church attendance, never using improper language or His name in vain, and a quiet time at least twice a week as minimums. Under "honoring each other" came the family rule that they weren't to talk back to their parents or dishonor any family member with their words. And under "honoring God's creation" came the various chores to keep the house presentable, as well as taking care of the family pets.

All families operate by rules. The problem is that in most homes, the rules are unwritten. And while we can't explain it completely, we've seen that when a family's rules are put in writing and followed consistently, less confusion and greater harmony come to that home.

After writing out their basic rules, the Murphys began applying the three keys to making a family contract work. First, right next to each rule they drew two columns, one for a reward if it was fulfilled, and another for a penalty if it wasn't. *Then the children were allowed to write in their own rewards and penalties, with guidance.*

Betty needed help from her parents in fitting the penalty to the failure when she suggested, "If I miss feeding the cat, how about if I'm grounded for two weeks?" After some discussion, it was agreed that missing television for one night was more realistic.

Sam needed help in making the reward section more realistic. If he remembered to feed the dog each day during the week without being asked, his first suggestion was that he wouldn't have to mow the yard for the entire summer. After some discussion, they all agreed that keeping the rule meant he could spend two hours on Saturday afternoon at the local mall. Failing to keep it meant no mall that weekend.

Perhaps you can see already what was beginning to happen around the Murphy home. Now, instead of every rule's being "Dad's rule" or "Mom's thing," they were the children's rules, too, complete with their own set of rewards and penalties. As ownership of the family rules went up, the kids' grounds for defying Mom and Dad went down. Fighting the rules soon became a way of fighting with themselves, and that wasn't nearly as much fun.

The second key to a successful contract was that *the children were allowed as much freedom as possible in meeting their specific responsibilities.* For example, the family members committed themselves to having at least ten minutes of "quiet time" twice a week. For Sam, this usually meant using the last ten minutes at night, reading some of the interesting stories and applications from *The Student Bible.*[3]

Of course, some rules were unbendable. There was no fudge factor if they used improper language or talked back in anger. However, flexibility about when the trash was taken out or when the dog was fed (any time before dark) again took away the need to nag. The children were also responsible for marking their own chores on the contract sheet if they wanted credit toward a reward that day. That put the responsibility back on the person whose chore it was, not on a parent to constantly remind Betty or Sam to get it done.

The third and most important key to an effective family contract system is something the best business leaders (and Ed and Doris) know: *You can expect what you take time to inspect.* The one meal the Murphy family could all count on having together was breakfast. So it was then that the parents took the contract sheet off the refrigerator to see what the children had checked off.

The first three weeks were a test for Mom and

Dad and Sam. He missed doing his chores on several days, which meant he couldn't go to the mall that weekend. He even had to come home early from his cousin's birthday party when everyone else was headed to a movie at the mall. ("Miss feeding the dog, miss going to the mall—at all.") But after Mom and Dad held firm during that testing period, which they had been told to expect, soon many positive things were happening.

Ed found he had boundaries around his anger now. Instead of yelling, pointing his finger at the kids, or feeling he had to be dramatic to show how serious he was, he could point to the contract on the refrigerator. It also helped him to remember that in addition to giving penalties for rule-breaking, he could motivate positively by giving rewards for good behavior.

Doris, our golden retriever, found strength to be more lovingly hardside than ever before because of having the rules right in front of her. As she looked at the contract, she could see the positive things the children could gain, and she also knew there were limits to the discipline if they failed in their tasks. All this gave her the confidence to stand firmer in providing the unified parental front her children had needed all along.

Finally, Sam the otter and Betty the beaver also began to thrive under this system. In spite of himself, Sam liked filling out the chart, especially checking off what he had done with a big marker. After several months, he even found himself making habits out of several areas of responsibility he had once hated. And for Betty, a contract system was pure heaven. At last, the family was getting organized like her, and she was being rewarded for doing everything just right.

You might wonder if the positive things that happened to the Murphy family were a one-time phenomenon. But the Smalley family enjoyed the same results. That's because the contract system we taught the Murphys was the same one the Smalleys used for years. In fact, I (Gary) credit that system we used while the children grew up for much of the close-knit unity we're experiencing today.

As you'll see in the next chapter, the most important key to a family contract's success is the hardside love to hold another person accountable. But as tough as it was to inspect the contract each day, it brought incredible softness to our home through the reduction of friction and the addition of love and respect.

Bringing family rules to light and putting them down on paper is one way for everyone to win.

We know you may have a number of practical questions on using contracts that we're not able to cover here. If you'd like to go deeper in learning this helpful method, see Gary's book *The Key to Your Child's Heart* or *Who's in Charge Here?* by Robert G. Barnes, Jr.

Now let's look at another way of adding softness that comes through awareness of a silent, hardside language.

6. Recognize the destructive power of nonverbal hardness.

The apostle James pointed out a way to be spiritually blessed by looking into a mirror. Wise people will look intently at who they are and make needed changes. But foolish people will look into that same mirror and walk away unchanged.[4]

How many times have you looked in the mirror today? This week? We may glance at our reflection ten times a day to help us look our best. But to act our best, we need to gaze into the mirror intently and even more often to see how others perceive us.

A counselor friend recently told us about a rather inventive wife. She just couldn't get through to her husband that one of her major concerns was not what he said to her, but the way he looked at her. She told the counselor that her husband rarely raised his voice, yet his angry and dishonoring gestures made her feel insecure and attacked. He could hold his tongue, but he couldn't control his gestures and sharp glances. When they were alone, his looks held an edge that could cut through cold steel.

Desperate to get through to her husband, she used a method we don't endorse because it could backfire, though it worked for her. She set up her own "Candid Camera," hiding their small video camera in the family room bookshelf and pointing it toward the kitchen, where many of their arguments took place. Then she turned it on the moment she heard his car in the garage.

We'll never be truly effective at
communicating the soft side of love if we
don't take a hard look at what we're saying
nonverbally.

That night, after another series of hardside looks
and gestures, she again confronted her husband.
And this time, she played back the tape so he could
see what concerned her.

What he saw wouldn't have made the first cut on
"America's Funniest Home Videos." But it could
have won first prize on "America's Most-Strained-
Out Couples." He was stunned as he watched how
many times he rolled his eyes back, tossed out his
hands as he tossed aside her words, and crossed his
arms or turned aside when she talked to him. All he
could say was, "Is that really me? Do I really look
that way?"

Researchers tell us that the vast majority of what
we say is nonverbal. From the tilt of our head to the
narrowing of our eyes to slamming a door, we
communicate volumes by what we don't say. *And
we'll never be truly effective at communicating the
soft side of love if we don't take a close look at what
we're saying nonverbally.*

Learning to be softer with others begins with our
eyes and mouths. If our brows are furrowed and
our mouths are tightly drawn, our words may be as
soft as a feather, but the person will be receiving a
hardside message. That's because *in a mixed message of soft words and hard nonverbal signals, all
ties go to the hard side.*

It's been said that one picture is worth a thousand words. And every time we talk to a person, our nonverbal clues are giving a clear picture of what we're really thinking.

The whole body gets involved in a frown. Take a moment and do this exercise. Put on your most disapproving face: eyes narrowed, teeth clenched, neck stiff—the kind of face you'd reserve for that teacher who always gave pop quizzes on Friday afternoon or the girl who broke up with you in ninth grade and wouldn't give back all the expensive stuff you'd bought her.

Now notice your breathing. Putting yourself in this nonverbal position will increase your heartbeat, make your breath become shallow, tighten your neck and stomach muscles, and in general put your whole body on the defensive.

Now try relaxing, and put on your widest smile. Could you feel your whole body relax? Your breathing automatically becomes deeper. If you could measure it, you'd also see that your pupils dilated slightly when you smiled, taking in more of your environment and assuming a warmer, more friendly appearance to others. "A cheerful look brings joy to the heart," the Bible tells us.[5]

The next time you're having a "serious" discussion with your spouse or child, try something that can help you as much as the most persuasive argument. Take a break from the intensity of the moment to smile and take a hand or give a hug, indicating that in spite of the issue you're facing, you still love the person.

We also need to be careful about our tone of

voice. It rarely lies about what we're really feeling when we talk with someone. Ask your loved ones for a regular tone-of-voice check to make sure some negative embedded emotions aren't erasing the positive effect of your words.

Nonverbal softness is at its best, however, not when we're talking but when we're listening. We can be sure we're communicating softness if our shoulders are pointed directly at the person and we're leaning forward just a bit. Taking the time to turn and squarely face another person also communicates warmth and attention, as does getting down at eye level with a child. But turning to the side or facing the stove or television can communicate hardness, even if that's not our intent.

Finally, use the nonverbal hardness of others to spot tension in your home. Not too long ago, it seemed that something was wrong with Norma. So I (Gary) decided to look at her nonverbal signals to try to isolate the problem.

First, I noticed that when we spoke, she often wouldn't look at me. Our conversations seemed short and to the point. She'd also cross her arms or sit on the other side of the couch. But every time one of our children came around, her eyes lit up, and she was ready to talk at any hour of the day or night. Finally, when I reached out toward her, she resisted closeness and tensed up whenever we hugged.

I didn't need to be a missile scientist to realize

her problem was with me! I finally found out that I'd been criticizing her over one particular area, and she'd had enough. She had never verbalized her frustration, but it was there to see in her actions.

Fortunately, by looking at her body language, I had quickly spotted her frustration. And by working at not being critical in that area, I soon had our relationship back on a positive note.

7. Become personally involved in helping others.

My (Gary's) daughter, Kari Lynn, is in the middle of her first year of teaching at an inner-city school. And while she has always had a compassionate heart, I've seen her develop an even deeper level of softness this year. Why? Because it's been a season of sacrificing for others, and it has really sensitized her heart.

Nearly all her students are Hispanic, and two of them started class speaking no English at all. I've watched her spend hours of her free time tutoring and encouraging her students to speak and read English better.

I don't say this to put a public spotlight on what she's done to help her students, but to point out the incredible way involvement with others softens hearts, even if it means sacrificing our time and resources. If you find your heart isn't as soft as it should be, ask yourself a question: Are you involved in a situation where you're serving others? Whether it's in the church nursery, taking a missions trip to Mexico, or at the local hospital, we can learn powerful lessons in softness by reaching out to others.

8. Allow tough times to mold us into soft people.

We know a couple on a church staff who have had to suffer the heartache of infertility. They've endured painful tests, various medications, and untold stress. For years, every toy store, every Sunday morning seeing all their friends' kids in the nursery, and every Christmas with only two stockings hung on the mantle were reminders of the emptiness they felt. But some of the most difficult times they experienced came at the hands of well-meaning church members.

On more than one occasion, the wife received notes from women who had children saying that she should accept and applaud "God's will" that they be childless. And often she was told how special, strong or blessed she must be for God to have given her such a burden. This couple didn't need lectures on God's will from people who couldn't relate to their pain, but sympathy, understanding and occasionally a shoulder to cry on.

Many people go through trials, but not all are trained by them. Physical pain or other problems can make us harder in our personal lives. Yet for this couple, and for many others who have gone through a season of difficulty, hard times can make soft people.

Some time ago, we had the opportunity to spend a week with Dr. Charles Swindoll and his church staff, speaking at their church's family camp. Since we were in the middle of our research on this book, it seemed a perfect time to ask one of the softest, warmest individuals we've met what his secret is to communicating so much genuine love for those in his flock.

Dr. Swindoll paused and wrinkled his brow. Finally, after a few moments, he gave a one-word answer: "Pain." Then he spoke of the pain of nearly losing his granddaughter, of doing funerals for too many close friends, of pouring his heart into people who wouldn't listen to biblical counsel, and of receiving unjustified criticism. Going through pain will make us either bitter or better. Charles Swindoll's trials have deepened and softened his love for Christ and for others.

Are trials making you harder, blocking softside love in the process? We believe that our response to pain and its effect on our ability to love is so important that we wrote a whole book about it: *Joy That Lasts.*

The apostle James told us that we're not to resent trials but welcome them as friends. And while that's not always easy to do, sharing in Christ's suffering is a sure way to gain a deeper sense of His love. It's also a powerful way of softening our hearts so that our love for others comes shining through.

9. Keep our hearts spiritually soft.

Without question, the greatest single way to soften our love for others is to increase our love for Christ. This is so important that we'll spend the entire last chapter of the book addressing it. But for now, we can do two things to keep our hearts spiritually soft.

First, we add softness by remaining open to correction from others. In the Scriptures we read, "A rebuke goes deeper into one who has understanding than a hundred blows into a fool."[6] In other words, wise people are soft and receptive to words of correction; fools are hardened to any attempts to point out their faults. And unfortunately, the less open we are, the more we harden our hearts toward God and others. Conversely, if we want to be wise, we need to remain soft toward what God can teach us through the correction of others.

Second, we add spiritual softness by not trafficking in those things that bring darkness to the heart. Romans 1 contains a long list of such things, including unrighteousness, wickedness, greed, evil, murder, strife, deceit, slander, hatred and especially sexual sin.

Without a doubt, the best way to add softness and keep darkness out is to live a godly life. Consider sexual sin, for example, which is epidemic in our society. One reason it darkens the heart is that it forces us to live two different lives. There's the public life of a devoted husband, wife, student or clergyman, yet there's also the secret life of trafficking in darkness.

The more we live as two very different people, the more we harden our hearts in a negative way toward God and others. Each time we push away the Holy Spirit's conviction of sin, refusing to repent, we invite our hearts to become more rock-hard. Time and again, we've seen that such an unfeeling heart can cause us to do and say things that would have been unimaginable only a few months before.

There's no question but that secret sins lead to a hardened heart. And all the time we're turning away from God, we're not really getting away with anything. As the psalmist said, "If we had forgotten the name of our God . . . would not God have discovered it, since he knows the secrets of the heart?"[7]

The more we walk in the truth, the less sin can act like slow-drying cement in our hearts and block our ability to give and receive both sides of love.

10. Make it your goal to be soft with those you love.

If you're a lion or beaver, goals feel as good as a hot towel right out of the dryer. When someone gives you a goal, the challenge fuels your fire. So with that in mind, we challenge you, here and now, to make it a goal to add softness to your love for others.

If you need to learn more about motivating your children based on their personality bents, we recommend the book *Tailor-Made Kids in an Off-the-Rack World,* by Jim Brawner. In this excellent resource, you'll see many ways to use both sides of love to inspire your kids.[8]

For the two of us, as of the time we're writing this, it's been almost two years since our wives sat us down and told us we needed to add more of this side of love to our lives. And for two years, it's become more and more of a conscious, daily goal. But such a decision comes at a cost. We still have the otter tendency to attack verbally when under stress. And our ideas of softness haven't always matched those of our wives and children. We've had to have family meetings to talk things out, and sometimes we've had to ask forgiveness for going back to what's comfortable, even if it is far out of balance.

We know it's not easy for a lion to take on characteristics of a lamb, but it's been done before. The book of Revelation is full of pictures of the Son of God who sits on His throne as both. And as we grow to be more like Him, we'll see softness increasing in our relationships with others.

Ten ways to add softness, and each has the power to enrich our relationships. But we also need the hard, protective side of love. And in the next two chapters, we'll look closely at ten ways to add more of that side if it's the missing part of a healthy balance.

10

Adding Hardside Love in a Healthy Way, Part I

It was pitch-dark as Steve stood in his daughter's room. *Perhaps I'm wrong,* he thought as he looked over the sleeping form of his daughter. *Everybody thinks I am. But Lord, I know I'm not. Please help me to stay strong.*

Steve would never be mistaken for a lion. It's not that he wasn't manly, but he was clearly at the far end of the golden retriever scale. He could be firm if he was pushed, but he was so flexible with others that he'd seldom had to use the hard side of love. Instead, he had always been the warm, supportive father who handed out more hugs and less discipline than the average dad.

As we've seen, softness is essential. Run down the biblical lists of the fruit of the Spirit and the character qualities of an elder or deacon, and half of them call for softsided love. But Steve needed now to apply the protection and correction of love's hard side. For a major problem had shown up at his door that softness alone couldn't handle.

In fact, Steve's worst nightmare had come true. While he had suspected it for several months, now he knew that his fifteen-year-old daughter, Robin, was doing drugs with her new friends at her new school. The guidance counselor had called in him and his wife when drugs were found hidden on top of the locker Robin shared. No charges had been filed because neither girl had been caught in direct possession, but an explosion went off in Steve's mind when he faced the facts.

He didn't know how involved Robin was, but he could no longer explain away her moody behavior and deceptive stories. He could tell he was losing his daughter to drugs, dead-end friends, and who knew what else, and he had to do something about it.

There are times when life calls us to take a stand, when strength has to be added to softness. In a move far out of character for Steve, he made several major decisions at once.

First, Robin would transfer to a different school. While drugs are on every high school campus, he felt strongly that she needed to make a break from this school. The same thing went for her newfound friends. She was to cut all ties with them, including phone calls or "accidental" meetings at the mall. (He chaperoned her to make sure of that.) Finally, they were going back to church, and she was to go into counseling, along with the rest of the family, beginning immediately.

You can imagine the impact these decisions had on the entire family. Robin was enraged and threatened to run away. Night after night, she refused to speak to him or even look at him unless forced to do so. Her younger sister, a golden retriever by temperament, responded to the hurt she saw in Robin's life and also attacked their father as being too harsh and cruel. Even his wife began to doubt him and wondered aloud if he had gone overboard with the whole situation.

Two months had now passed, and Robin was in her new school, away from the old friends. It was past midnight, and once again, Steve had been unable to sleep, tossing and turning with his stomach tied in knots as he struggled with conflicting emotions. *Am I being too hard? Have I gone overboard?* he thought. At last, he decided to do the only thing that seemed to give him any comfort; he was going downstairs to pray.

But this night, on his way to the stairs, Steve stopped by Robin's room. The door was half open, and he peered into the darkness. After a moment of letting his eyes adjust, he stepped inside and watched her sleep.

Emotions gripped him as he remembered all the nights he had stood there when she was young, looking down on her as she held her blanket or a favorite stuffed animal. He recalled how she used to smile whenever he walked into a room. But now he felt only hatred from her, and it was tearing his heart to pieces.

Tears filled his eyes as he started to turn away. And then his daughter spoke. "Daddy?" she said. "Is that you?"

He stopped where he was and turned slowly. "Yes, Honey," he said.

After a long pause, he could tell his daughter had begun to cry softly. "Daddy," she said, "thank you for loving me. I was stuck, and I didn't know how to get out. Thank you for being firm with me . . ."

Steve had paid a tremendous price to hear those words. There is no anger like that of a person who is caught up in darkness and then forced to look at the light. Steve even had to shoulder the anger of others who felt he was overreacting and cruel.

Tough love isn't easy, and it often doesn't bring rewards in just two months. We know other people who have had to be hard with a loved one and seen a child or spouse walk away for years. But one thing is certain: Had Steve decided to give only the soft side of love to his daughter, he would never have won back her love, and he might have lost her forever.

This chapter is for all of us who have struggled with being too soft in our love for others—people like Steve who lean toward the soft side, who need a healthy hardness to balance their love not just in a crisis, but every day.

It's our otter and golden retriever friends who tend to camp out on the soft side of love. Being naturally soft on people, they're often too soft on problems as well. To see just how well you fit that description, go down the following softness survey, answering yes or no to each question.

1. Do you tend to hold your feelings inside rather than express them to others? _____

2. Can you criticize a friend? _____

3. Can you ask others for a favor or ask for help with a problem you're having? _____

4. Do you have difficulty saying no to an added responsibility, even when you know you're overcommitted? _____

5. Do you leave most of the discipline of the children to your spouse? _____

6. When someone compliments you, do you feel uncomfortable or have to explain it away? _____

7. Are most of your times with friends spent listening to their needs and concerns, without voicing your own? _____

8. Do you feel that being aggressive and being assertive are basically the same thing? _____

9. Do you often walk away from confrontations with your children and feel, deep inside, that they've won again? _____

10. Was it difficult for you to express anger in your home growing up? _____

11. Do you feel that your spouse is being too hard

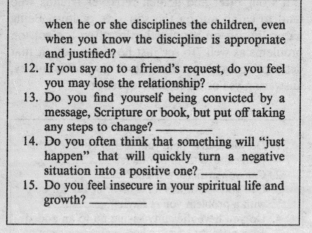

when he or she disciplines the children, even
when you know the discipline is appropriate
and justified? _____

12. If you say no to a friend's request, do you feel
you may lose the relationship? _____

13. Do you find yourself being convicted by a
message, Scripture or book, but put off taking
any steps to change? _____

14. Do you often think that something will "just
happen" that will quickly turn a negative
situation into a positive one? _____

15. Do you feel insecure in your spiritual life and
growth? _____

If you had more yes answers than you have
fingers on one hand, this chapter is definitely for
you. You're on the low side of the hardside scale
and will really benefit from what follows. But even
those who answered no fifteen times can learn a
great deal about how to be hardside in a healthy,
balanced way.

Where do we begin? Just as in the last chapter, by
blasting before we build. For as important as it is to
spot emotional freeze points that can block softness, it's equally important to see how they can
shut off hardside love.

1. Recognize the effect of emotional freeze points.

The year was 1951, and Sergeant Davis's part of
the Korean War had just ended. When the war
began, his reserve unit was one of the first called

into active duty. The Army had paid his way through college. In return, for twelve months and eleven days, he paid the Army back the hard way: fighting up and down the freezing mountains and hills, often with fixed bayonet, near the thirty-eighth parallel.

Sergeant Davis was now just plain old Dad to Margie, his nine-year-old daughter. But one night soon after his return from the war, he put back on his stripes in an incident he would never forget.

It was bedtime, and Margie had asked for a glass of milk and some cookies before turning in. She was laughing and clowning around in the kitchen when she knocked over her glass, shattering it and spilling milk all over the floor.

The late hour, the loud noise and his over-wrought nerves from having recently been in a war zone combined to cause Margie's father to forget whom he was talking to. Instinctively, he reamed her out with a tongue-lashing fit for a disobedient soldier. Shocked by his harshness and vulgarity, Margie burst into tears.

Unfeelingly, he shouted at her, "Get down the hall and get to bed." Then he stormed outside as she fled to her room.

"It was her that broke the glass, not me," he said defiantly to his wife when she came out later to talk to him. He refused to go in and apologize to Margie, ending the discussion with a halfhearted admission, "All right, I was a little hard on her. But she'll forget it." Only she didn't.

Later that night, terrible screams came from

Margie's room. Davis rushed into her bedroom and found her sitting straight up in bed, soaked in sweat and crying uncontrollably.

"What's wrong?" he said, putting his arm around her as she shook with fear.

"Oh, Daddy, it was terrible," she said. "There was this bear, and he was attacking me. He kept clawing me, and he wouldn't stop."

It took nearly a half hour of gently rocking her before she was willing to try to go back to sleep. And even then, she insisted a small light be left on in the room. Just before he left, a thought struck Davis like a blow to the gut.

"I wasn't a Christian at the time," he said later, "but I felt even then that the Lord was forcing me to realize what I'd done." Turning to his daughter, he asked, "Honey, was the bear in your dreams Daddy?"

The nodding of her little head told him all he needed to know. He hugged her and asked her forgiveness for being so harsh with her.

Ex-Sergeant Davis, today Dr. Davis, later told us that night was a watershed event in his life. It would change the way he related not only to Margie, but also to each of the children who came later.

"As I reached the door and looked back on my daughter lying in bed," he said, "I couldn't believe what I'd done. I made a decision right then that I would never, ever, be harsh with my daughter like that. I would never make her feel like I was a bear again."

That decision became an emotional freeze point. The picture of his daughter, sitting up in bed and screaming in fear, was so vivid to him over the years that it pushed him far to the soft side of love. And while that was a positive outcome in many ways, it also had its drawbacks. By blocking off the hard side of love, he also pushed nearly all the discipline responsibilities onto his wife.

Dr. Davis isn't alone. Over the years, we've spoken with a number of people who have experienced an event or season that blocked them from expressing love's hard side. I (Gary) have also seen it in my own family.

I'm the last of five children, and just before I came along, my mother went through such a freeze point. I had an older sister named Lorna, who was five at the time. As my mother later told the story, Lorna had done something wrong and had been disciplined for it, including my mother's giving her a swat with a kitchen spoon.

While my mother didn't know it at the time, several days before, Lorna had picked up a splinter in her arm while playing outside. It was already sore, but soon an infection set in. And without the powerful antibiotics we have today, the infection spread too quickly for the doctors to catch, and Lorna died in my mother's arms.

The spanking had played no part in my sister's death, but never again would my mother discipline any of us children, nor would she let my father. She was devastated by losing her daughter, and the memory of her spanking Lorna just before she got so sick added a layer of guilt to the terrible pain.

I don't blame my mother for not being able to show this side of love. But I do know that the lack of discipline in my home affected me in several ways. For example, I had difficulty accepting rules for a long time because I never had to follow them at home. And it wasn't just me. I saw it affect my brothers, and especially my sister, in a negative way as well.

For many of us, however, our natural softside bent wasn't pushed to an extreme by something in the past; it's just always been there. We were the ones to take chicken soup to the sick or to be called for a favor in the middle of the night. If that description fits you, the next method of adding hardness will be important for you to see.

2. Allow a short time of distance to build a season of closeness.

In chapter 8 we included a survey to help you see how close or distant you tend to be in your important relationships. Take a moment to review your results. Scoring high on the closeness scale can signal a very positive relationship. But it may also point out a possible problem when it comes to expressing the hard side of love.

By nature, otters and golden retrievers tend to be very strong at building relationships. But if those close relationships develop problems, they're apt to explain them away, "give them more time to work out," or try to ignore what's wrong altogether.

Why? It's a classic case of people's strengths being pushed to an extreme and becoming their greatest weaknesses.

Time and again in this book, we've encouraged you to be hard on problems and soft on people. For many otters and golden retrievers, however, there's a basic problem in doing that. *They get so close to people that they can't separate the person from the problem. So they begin to equate legitimate correction with personal rejection.*

I (John) have certainly experienced this. My family was very close as I was growing up. However, in many ways, we were so close that I never learned to separate what people did from who they were. The focus was so much on personal acceptance (who we were, not what we did) that to attack a problem was to attack the person. And that inability to accept healthy correction proved to be a problem later on.

The most insecure people are those who can't distance themselves from their loved ones far enough to discipline them.

After I married Cindy and our daughter was born, I found myself repeating the patterns I'd experienced at home. Much of what I passed on was good. But I also struggled with disciplining our daughter because somehow, deep inside, it felt as if correcting her was a way of saying I didn't accept or love her.

Thankfully, Cindy is a beautiful example of the

balance I didn't grow up with. She loves Kari deeply, but she doesn't confuse disapproving of her actions with not accepting her as a person. She can be firm and put limits on her behavior, because she has enough emotional distance to separate the person from the problem.

That's one reason Kari loves Cindy so much and a large part of why she was an outstanding teacher for a number of years. Her students always knew they were deeply loved, but they also knew the rules. And they knew she was strong enough to keep them, even if that meant that for a short time there was some distance in the relationship.

The most insecure people are those who can't distance themselves from their loved ones far enough to discipline them. They fear that if they confront a child or spouse, they'll lose the relationship, or at least the *feelings* that go with it. Even if it's only for a short time and for the other person's good, they think confronting the person will be like pulling the rug out from under their relationship.

Actually, their fear is justified. As the Scriptures say, no child likes to be disciplined. After correction, there normally is a period of emotional distance between the parent and child. That's what makes it particularly hard for golden retrievers to confront. They can't stand being separated from their loved ones emotionally, even if it's only for a short time. But genuine love recognizes that not to lance a boil or give children the medicine they need—even if they don't want it or like us for it—isn't really loving at all.

Loving discipline may put an emotional distance between people for a few hours or, as in Steve's case, a few months. It's only natural and shouldn't be feared. If we balance that hardside correction with softness, we won't lose love. If anything, we'll enrich it.

Thus far, we've looked at two ways to increase hardside love. Now let's look at a third—learning a single word that can go a long way toward strengthening our most-important relationships.

3. Learn to use a word that can save your relationships.

It's hard to imagine the incredible power of a single word. We've seen people take or lose control of their lives simply by saying or failing to say this one hardside word: *no.* It's one of the first words we learn as children, and most of us become experts at using it repeatedly by the time we're two. But sometime between age two and our twenties, many of us lose the ability to say it.

Golden retrievers and otters have particular difficulty saying no. It's almost as if they have a genetic defect that doesn't allow their tongues to move away from the top of their mouths to complete the word. Instead, they start to say no, but it comes out, "Nnn—oh, okay."

We all know people who struggle with saying no. There's the loving mother who has to make at least one trip to the high school each day to bring her son something he's forgotten: his football jersey, his tennis shoes or his lunch. She understands she should say no to a senior who ought to be learning to be responsible for himself, but she just can't do it.

Then there's the person who can't say no to another volunteer job, even if it means missing time with the family, and the pastor who adds "just one more counseling session" to his packed schedule because he's called to the ministry, after all.

It's helpful to realize that Jesus said no. He said no when asked to come heal Lazarus. Instead, He waited right where He was for three days, and Lazarus died. Jesus said no to being crowned king by the mob, knowing His reign on earth would be at His next coming. He said no to His disciples when they asked to sit at His right hand, and He said no to His accusers when they baited Him to answer their unjust charges. Jesus said no often, and He had good reasons for doing so.

Of course, that doesn't mean we should say no to everything. If we really believe something is important, we may need to say yes, even if it costs us time and effort. But there are at least five reasons we should be able to say no, as Christ did, and draw on the hard side of love to do so.

Failing to say no can allow unwanted attitudes to take root in our homes. We hate to say it, but some parents in particular should be charged with contributing to the delinquency of a minor. By failing to say no to their children, they're building a learned helplessness and, to some degree, a level of irresponsibility within their kids.

Children are smart. If Mom or Dad will do it for

them, why should they pick up their rooms, do their homework for themselves, learn to save money instead of spending it, or practice other responsibilities they'll need later in life? It's difficult to say no to kids and have them accept the consequences of their actions. But at times, they need the hard side of love to help them build positive habits and avoid negative ones.

Failing to say no can keep us from doing what's really important. Time and again, we've seen people who can't say no to what's important to someone else, and they end up sacrificing what's really important in their own homes.

Take Mark, for example. His otter need to be liked by others at work meant he spent a good deal of time helping them with their jobs. He took on so many tasks that should have been on other people's desks, never refusing a request, that he couldn't get to all that was on his own. He often had to take his work home just to stay caught up, robbing him of time that should have been reserved for his family.

People who can't say no usually get so caught up in the urgent needs of other people that they miss out on what's really important in their own lives—things like quiet times, time with their children and meeting household responsibilities.

Failing to say no can allow tension and resentment to build up. Doris was a new teacher, and for nearly a year, her "initiation" consisted of having her principal give her all the jobs nobody wanted. Feeling she had no say in the matter, she accepted the extra lunch, playground and bus duties that were laid on her. But while she took each additional assignment with hardly a word, inside she was screaming at herself and him and feeling used.

Finally, near the end of the school year, she blew up in the principal's office when he added yet another assignment. "Doris," he said with surprise written all over his face, "if you're overloaded, all you had to do was tell me. I'll get someone else to do it."

As a loyal golden retriever, she thought saying no to her principal would be a personal affront to him. If she hadn't cared so much for the school and her job, it might have been easier to say no. But her natural depth of involvement made her accept anything handed to her until she finally reached the breaking point. It also made her so resentful toward her principal that it affected her sleep, her diet and her attitude toward work. Yet all the time she was carrying around such a burden, she never once expressed those feelings until she nearly snapped.

People who hold in their frustration and fail to be hard with others when it's needed pay a price—in some cases, much too high a price.

When I (Gary) was on the staff of a large organization several years ago, I supervised a man I'll call Dennis. He was an expert in his field, but he was just as much an expert at avoiding any kind of confrontation. He hated to say no to anyone, and he couldn't bring himself to correct those who worked for him.

Dennis had an employee who spent too much

time socializing on the job. This employee was very likable, but he just didn't know when to stop talking and start working. To make matters worse, the head of our organization often saw him stop working and make small talk with anyone who walked by. After a while, it became so irritating to the boss that he brought it to my attention. He asked me to have Dennis, the man's supervisor, address the problem, which meant I had to call in "Never Say No" Dennis.

In a gentle way, I told him about the problem and gave him some suggestions for handling it. On several occasions when I brought it up again, he assured me he'd take care of it. But he never did.

Failing to say no can cut meaningful
communication in half.

I tried everything I knew to help him deal with his fear of confronting this employee. We talked, we role-played, I encouraged, he promised, and still nothing ever happened. He just couldn't face the situation and say, "No, you can't take a break whenever someone walks by." This became such a major issue that it put his manager's job in jeopardy and subjected him to incredible stress.

As it turned out, Dennis developed serious health problems that were stress-related, according to his doctor. He soon retired, and he died as a result of those complications only a few years later. I'm sure Dennis wasn't aware at the time of the high price he was paying for failing to deal with problems. When he finally found out that bottling his fear and frustration inside was unhealthy, it was too late.

One of the biggest hurdles a softside person faces is being willing to confront others and say no. In fact, a number of top-notch Christian counselors have told us that *it's much easier to get a hardside person to become softer than it is to get a softside person to become harder.* It's almost as if there's an emotional trip switch that shuts down a softside person's attempts to confront, and especially to say no.

Failing to say no can cut meaningful communication in half. As Dennis's case shows, when people refuse to face a difficult situation (like telling a person no), they shut off the important discussion that can go with voicing their real feelings.

One reason people have difficulty saying no is that it begs questions in return. For example, if you tell your teenage daughter, "No, you can't go to that movie," what will you instantly hear? "But why, Mother? Everyone else is going."

What we often don't realize is that by not saying no, we miss some of the most important teaching times we'll ever have with others. We may avoid a heated discussion today, but we also lose the opportunity to say something that may affect the rest of their lives.

Not long ago, I (Gary) found it necessary to say no to one of our employees. He's so good at his job that other ministries and companies kept asking him to do work for them. Soon his talent was being used more for outside projects than for those within our organization, Today's Family.

As an otter, I like positive, friendly relationships, which is a nice way of saying I don't like to tell people no. I put off confronting him about what was happening for several months, thinking he'd see the problem himself or that the requests would just stop coming in. But he never did and they never stopped, and all the time I was growing more resentful.

While I don't struggle in being hard with my spouse and children, at the office I tend to be too soft with others. Finally, I realized *I* was the one paying the emotional price for not confronting him, and I brought him into my office and explained my concerns.

We had such a positive meeting that I couldn't believe I had been avoiding the conversation for months. He instantly saw the problem when I pointed it out and cut back nearly 100 percent on outside projects while we were so swamped with our own. By being willing to enter into a hardside discussion, I not only unloaded a ton of personal stress, but I also gained back a valuable employee.

Failing to say no can keep others and ourselves from the truth. Most of us are familiar with a term that current TV talk shows and self-help books have popularized: *codependency.* This word describes the way Martha learned to live with her alcoholic husband.

Martha was a perfect grandmother type: always there for the children, always ready to babysit their kids when they came along. Her only problem was that she was always making excuses for her husband's behavior.

Don was an alcoholic who maintained his job but who also put away several six-packs each night, and more on the weekend. If softside love alone could change a person, Martha's love would have changed Don. But it didn't. And as the years passed and his drinking became more of a problem, she found herself becoming an expert at uttering white lies.

She would tell her children about the "business that came up" so that their father couldn't make the family reunion; or that he "came down with something" and would have to drop by to see the new baby another day.

The only one Martha was fooling was herself, but the children pretended she was fooling them, too. It's not that Martha liked being a liar. But her out-of-balance softside love made protecting her husband and keeping peace in the family seem more important than the truth.

We've heard softside people say, "Sure, I'd like to go to that movie," when they really don't want to and know they shouldn't. We've seen others excuse a friend's behavior by saying, "Oh, he'll pay me back. He just needs a little more time." And much too often, we've seen people like Martha who, in the interest of protecting a husband, effectively prevented a cure.

These people don't think of themselves as liars, but their failure to give both sides of love to people who need both makes them so. The Gospel of John contains a verse that sounds soft and easy but can actually be very hard: "You will know the truth, and the truth will set you free."[1] Unfortunately, many people are missing the freedom of walking in the truth. They're afraid of exercising the kind of love that can face a problem, because they're afraid of saying, "No, this is wrong, and I need to deal with it."

We think we've made our case for the need to utter this small but incredibly important hardside word that can do so much to strengthen relationships. But how do you get a golden retriever to become more of a watchdog, or an otter to gain the strength of a lion?

Certainly it begins by practicing saying no. Dr. Howard Hendricks, a noted Christian educator and one of my (John's) seminary professors, had seen my natural otter bent toward pleasing people. And in a discipleship class I had with him, he gave me this excellent advice: "John, practice saying no to at least one thing a day. Even if it's just refusing a second piece of pie, get in a habit that can help you the rest of your life!"

So far, we've looked at three methods for adding hardside love to our lives. In the next chapter, we'll look at seven more ways, beginning with one that addresses perhaps the most common struggle of softsided people.

11

Adding Hardside Love in a Healthy Way, Part II

Tim knew he was in deep trouble. Marcy wasn't just talking about leaving this time, she was doing something. The voice of a divorce attorney on their answering machine, returning her call, didn't change into harmless chatter no matter how many times he replayed the message. Sadly, it was an inability to tap into the hard side of love that had brought Tim to the brink of divorce.

Marcy had been attracted to his sensitive heart right off in high school, and they had married within a year of graduation. But as time went by, his softness became less and less appealing, particularly because whenever real problems came up, he lacked the strength to face them.

Tim bounced from job to job, always working beneath his abilities and bringing in far less than their needs. He was great at starting a new job, but he couldn't stay with one once it became routine. Marcy didn't mind working. But soon it was apparent that if she didn't work, even after the children came along, they wouldn't eat.

With each job change, Tim's self-confidence inched downward and his weight upward. Always he sought for some new thing, some opportunity that would instantly lift him out of his predicament. The state lottery drawing was always a high point in his week. He just knew that one day he would win the jackpot, and everything would change—even though his chances of winning were less than those of being hit twice by lightning.

That "something" he looked for to bail him out of having to change never came. And after nearly twenty years of marriage, they had finally reached rock bottom. Marcy had become so frustrated waiting for him to take the first step toward self-confidence and a decent job that she was ready to take the last step in contacting a lawyer.

Why could Tim, like so many people, see clearly what he needed to do, yet that first step seemed a mile high? Why couldn't he become more self-disciplined and spiritually strong, adding the hard side of love to his natural softness?

Tim was facing one of the greatest barriers to making needed inner adjustments. Whether the need is to take on the strength of hardside love or to become softer, the future of our relationships could well depend on our ability to make those changes. Yet it often seems as if a pair of giant arms holds us back until the opportunity for change has passed us by.

When pushed to an extreme, as easily happens, procrastination has the power to put people out of work, freeze them in sin, and confine them to frustration and hopelessness.

That major barrier to change can be summed up in one word, *procrastination*. Overcoming it is the fourth way to add a healthy hardness to our lives. It may sound like an innocent problem on the surface. We all procrastinate at times, don't we? But when pushed to an extreme, as easily happens, procrastination has the power to put people out of work, freeze them in sin, and confine them to frustration and hopelessness.

That's why we can't afford to put off looking at the giant that procrastination can become. And while it certainly can strike a lion or beaver, softside people are particularly vulnerable to it. We'll look at procrastination from three different angles and see three practical ways to overcome it.

Take it from two authors who have spent years in personal research on procrastination and who put off working on this chapter until the last: learning to defeat this giant can go a long way toward enriching our relationships. And take it from Tim:

if he could learn to defeat this problem—which he did—you can, too.

4. Face the heart of procrastination.

How would you like to wear the title "World's Greatest Procrastinator"? No, it's not a title your spouse can win! It doesn't even go to those men whose names were on the front page of our local newspaper recently, the ten worst procrastinators in the entire city when it comes to paying child support.

Those men may grab an unfavorable limelight for a short time. But that's nothing compared to the most publicized procrastinator in history, Felix. He was a Roman governor, and since his story is recorded in the world's best-selling book, the Bible, he's history's best-known procrastinator. We can learn a lot about the problem by looking at his experience in the book of Acts.

The apostle Paul had been captured by the Jewish leaders of his day and brought before Felix. They wanted Paul put to death, but Felix was interested in hearing what this man had to say, so he had him brought before him. "As Paul discoursed on righteousness, self-control and the judgment to come, Felix was afraid and said, 'That's enough for now! You may leave. When I find it convenient, I will send for you.'"[1]

Paul's words brought the conviction that Felix needed to change certain areas in his life. But then as now, *conviction only points out the changes we need to make. It doesn't make them for us.* And something short-circuited the change process. Did you notice it in the Scripture? After hearing about righteousness, self-control and the judgment to come, Felix *became frightened.*

The four-letter word that lies at the heart of procrastination is *fear.* And whenever we put off needed inner changes, at least six types of fear can be holding us back.

The first of these is *fear of discipline.* Tim feared becoming disciplined more than he feared doing nothing. He didn't want to hear about the need for self-control, because he knew it meant saying no to appetites he didn't want to stop feeding. That's true for many people who "can't" exercise, read the Scriptures, share their faith, or confront a problem person or situation. They fear becoming rigid or too rule-conscious, so they avoid the hardside discipline that can actually give them rest.

A second fear causing procrastination is *fear of failure.* For some people, the possibility of failure is so threatening that they never begin a project or try to make changes. This is particularly true of those who tend to be perfectionists. As far as they're concerned, it's better to do nothing and not face the risk of failure than to try and fall short. That was part of Tim's problem. While he looked and acted unkempt and unorganized, he actually scored high on the beaver scale. But he didn't want to try for a really good job and be found lacking.

A third fear that holds people back is the *fear of success.* Some people fear changing because success would put them in the spotlight, and they want to stay on the sidelines. Others are plagued by guilt or feelings of inferiority and think they don't deserve success. They find ways to explain or push it away even if it does come to them.

Still others fear that success will bring rejection. We know a bright young woman who won a scholarship to attend a local college. Yet after two semesters, she had stopped attending classes and flunked out. Why? She was the only one from her family to go to college. Deep inside, she feared that each step she took toward academic success was another step away from her loved ones.

Others fear success because they think that once a level of achievement is reached, it will mean there's another peak, just a little higher, that they'll have to climb next. And some fear success because they know that finally achieving a long-sought goal could leave them feeling empty and without purpose.

A few years ago, we were asked to counsel with an extremely successful person who had just won his industry's highest honor. Instead of thrilling him, it sent him into a deep depression. He had lived for this prize, but like living for anything less than the Source of life, once he had it, he was left empty and miserable inside.

A fourth fear leading to procrastination is *fear of finding out our limitations*. Procrastination allows people to take comfort in believing their ability is greater than their performance. It's more tolerable to blame themselves for being disorganized or lazy than to feel that they're inadequate or unworthy. Tim would have made an excellent support person or second-in-command. But he kept trying and failing to get the top spot with a company instead of admitting his skills lay in production, not management.

A fifth fear causing procrastination is *fear of commitment.* We spoke once with a man who didn't want help. He was a terrible husband and father, and perhaps the only positive thing we could say about him was that he was honest about why he was leaving his wife and children.

"Frankly, I *know* what it takes to have a strong family," he said, "and I'm not willing to pay that price." He knew that a commitment to his family would mostly take *time* for his wife and kids. And he was so totally consumed with career and financial success that he feared what such a commitment would cost him in dollars more than he feared losing his family.

The sixth fear is *fear of being controlled.* For Felix, and for anyone who procrastinates in response to spiritual challenges, this last form of fear is often the first in line. Many people rightly sense the loss of control that comes with putting themselves totally in God's hands. And if the fear is strong enough, when God knocks on the door of their hearts, they slam it shut.

When we become frightened and put off changing, usually there's a moral problem we're struggling with, not an intellectual one. It's not that we don't understand what God is asking us to do, it's that we *do* understand. We just don't want to turn away from what we're pursuing and go in His direction. Felix wanted to hear about Jesus, but he didn't want Him to get close enough to change him. Tim rarely missed a Sunday morning at church, but he knew in his heart that his greatest fear was of giving himself totally to the Lord.

As you can see, two or more of these six types of fear can easily combine to block a person's ability to make needed changes—something we should know from reading the Bible. "Perfect love drives out fear" is a familiar statement from 1 John 4:18. But the reverse is true as well. Those who allow fear to control their lives actually become less and less loving.

What do we do when we realize we're putting off becoming more tough or tender?

The first thing is to face the fear. Pick an area you're procrastinating in right now. Perhaps you're a lion and you need to become more of a golden retriever with your children—more supportive of them and less demanding. Or you may be an otter who has started a hundred projects this year, but you need to add enough beaver qualities to finish some of them and save your job in the process. Perhaps you're a retriever like Tim who needs to stay put in one job rather than making monthly changes.

What's holding you back from making those changes? The first thing is undoubtedly fear. And facing which type of fear has a hold on you can be the first step in defeating it. What's the next step?

It's actually the fifth in our series of ten steps toward adding healthy hardness to your life.

5. Avoid the trap of relying on instant change.

If fear is the fuel that causes us to put off needed changes, the hope of instant, easy change adds a turbocharger to the problem. Nearly every day, something or someone would convict Tim that he needed to become more assertive, more forceful, more consistent, more disciplined, more of a spiritual leader—all hardside traits. But he was never moved to action. Yet in the hope of instantly getting enough money to cover up his need for change, he couldn't buy lottery tickets fast enough. Likewise, codependent Marsha held on to the dream that one day her husband would wake up cured of his alcoholism instead of in a drunken stupor.

The problem with basing your life on such a dream is that one day you'll have to wake up—guaranteed. At any time during his twenty years of marriage, Tim could have taken a steady job and earned those things he wanted for Marcy one by one. But it was easier to hold on to the dream that one lottery ticket, one marketing scheme, one *something* would turn everything around—until his dream shattered when he heard the divorce lawyer's message on the answering machine.

We wish there were an easy way to change, but any hardside or softside trait we need to add will only make its way into our lives the old-fashioned way—by earning it in daily persistence.

Experts say it takes at least twenty-one days of repeating something before it becomes a habit. We don't just wake up one morning with a newfound ability to correct our children lovingly, stand up to a spouse, or confront a friend. These hardside skills come through the toughness of character that cements them, one by one, into the center of our lives. And a great way to start that process is with the next concept.

6. Allow yourself to become accountable to others.

When Cindy and I (John) were first married, I scored near the top in the otter scale and near the bottom everywhere else. My graph looked like an EKG chart with one spike. That meant I was basically friendly, fun-loving, soft on people—and much too soft on responsibilities like balancing our checkbook.

During the first years of our marriage, I took procrastination to new heights (or depths) as month after month I put off balancing our checkbook until the very last minute. Forget the fact that I was married to a beaver who could probably run her own accounting firm. I was the "Big Kahuna" of this family, and I wasn't about to let a few bounced checks stop me from my unsuccessful but easy method of accounting.

My method was similar to the one described by our good friends Chuck and Barb Snyder in their extremely helpful book *Incompatibility: Grounds for a Great Marriage* (Questar, 1988). This (thankfully) little-used accounting procedure is to wait until the bank statement comes in and then simply cross off the balance in your checkbook, write in their balance, close your checkbook, and you're finished! (After all, the people at the bank have been to business school and have computers!)

Where this approach will lead you (besides the poorhouse) is into doing what I did regularly: change banks. That way I finally knew, at least for a short time, exactly what our balance was.

As you can imagine, my fiscal irresponsibility was causing great stress for my wife. And unfortunately, I couldn't print new money to get out of my problems the way our government does.

I'm happy to say I eventually stopped procrastinating in this area, and what made it possible is the most powerful method we know of defeating the problem: accountability. We've looked in the Scriptures and through every book we could find on the subject, and we've concluded that loving accountability is God's *primary* tool to stop a person from procrastinating and start making needed hardside or softside changes. Watch how it happened in my life.

Loving accountability is God's primary tool
to stop a person from procrastinating and
start making needed changes.

When we moved to Arizona from Texas, I joined a small group of men in an accountability group at our church. The group had three otters in it, including me, and one beaver, a man named Doug

Childress, to stop a person from procrastinating and start making needed changes.

When we started the group, we otters would all say the same thing about our spiritual and family lives: How was it going that week? Great! After a few weeks of the three otters meeting and high-fiving each other at breakfast over what a great job we were doing, Doug decided to do something beavers do best: inspect things.

I'll never forget the first night Doug called the house and asked to speak to—Cindy. That's when he asked her, "How's John doing as a husband and father?" and "Are there any areas he needs to work on that I could help hold him accountable for?"

You can imagine how much trouble I got in after that first call. But it wouldn't be the last. Doug was lovingly committed to me as a friend, so much so that he held me accountable week after week. And soon, in spite of myself, I found myself adding more beaver characteristics to my life—like balancing the checkbook the right way and seeing my relationship with Cindy improve as a result. I even started calling his wife, Judie, and asking how *he* was doing as a husband.

Is there someone who can be a Doug Childress to you, someone who can ask the hard questions, not to hurt you, but to help and encourage you? Remember, only the wise seek accountability, while fools resist correction. No one enjoys having a friend point out a weakness, but if it's done in a loving way for our best, even the strong arms of procrastination will begin to weaken. We all need someone who, "as iron sharpens iron,"[2] can chip away at the rough edges of our lives.

Dealing with procrastination isn't the only way of adding important hardside traits to our lives. The seventh method we'll look at taps into the natural strength of an otter and golden retriever to pave the way for our loved ones to accept our being hardside with them.

7. Build relational bridges to carry hardside words.

Otters and golden retrievers are great at building relational bridges. They enjoy closeness with others and can in no time build a secure environment of warmth and mutual respect. That skill is crucial to expressing the hard side of love to others. As a familiar Bible verse points out, "Faithful are the wounds of a friend, but deceitful are the kisses of an enemy."[3]

Have you ever met people who are so hard that they think this verse means wounding you *makes* them your friend? That's not what it means. Rather, it's in getting close to others that we can say the most difficult things and have them be taken in a faithful, loving way.

We can't encourage you enough to form strong, intimate relationships by using all the nurturing skills of the soft side of love. For in doing this, you'll be building the strongest bridge to carry loving hardside words when they need to be said. Lions and beavers especially need to work at this. And without question, the best way we know to convey hardside messages softly is to use word pictures. That's why we wrote an entire book explaining how they work *(The Language of Love).*

Otters and golden retrievers need to understand something important as well, however. Once those bridges of friendship have been built, we need to cross them when it's called for. Let us illustrate what we mean.

Shortly after I (John) graduated from seminary and had taken my first job as an assistant pastor, I was asked to do premarital counseling with a young couple. They were sure they were meant for each other, and they wanted me to perform their wedding. After meeting with them four times, I was sure I was being conned. They may have felt ready for marriage, but they were immature and had serious personal problems. As I found out later, they were also practicing immorality in spite of assuring me they weren't.

But her father was a long-standing member of the church, the invitations had already been sent out, and the church had been reserved. So, to my shame, I let the pressure of the moment set aside my concerns about performing the service. I should have told the couple, "No, I can't do the wedding, and you shouldn't find anyone else to do it, either, until much time and counseling have passed." Only I didn't.

In our counseling sessions, I had definitely built a bridge of friendship and respect with this couple. But when it came to expressing the hard side of love as I needed to, I never crossed that bridge. And less than a year later, I learned from her father one Sunday morning that they were getting a divorce.

Pastors are not infallible, and it was, after all, the first couple I'd ever counseled. But I knew in my heart that those were just excuses for failing to be lovingly hard.

I learned a great deal from that experience. I still use my softside bent to build bridges with the many couples I counsel in the premarital class at our church. But I now force myself to cross the bridge and say the hard things I need to, even if it's, "I'm sorry, but you shouldn't get married."

8. Break hardside changes down into bite-size steps.

Debbie was the frustrated mother of a junior higher. She knew she needed to be more hardside with her daughter in several areas. But as a golden retriever, she had never been hard with anyone before.

We helped Debbie break down into concrete steps the changes she wanted to see in her daughter. First we asked her to pick one area where she felt she needed to be more hardside with her child. Instantly, she said she was tired of having the house look as if a tornado had hit it every time her daughter came home from school.

Next we asked Debbie to write down just what her daughter did before and after school that frustrated her in this area. After a week of keeping notes, she brought in a list of almost thirty things. We boiled that down to three things she really wanted the girl to do when she hit the door: take her books and clothes to her room; clean up any dishes or utensils she used when she had a snack; and keep the stereo below ear-piercing level.

At that point, it wouldn't have worked simply to tell Debbie, "Now be more hardside with your daughter about these things." Instead, all three of them were put into a written family contract such as we discussed earlier. It took some time and encouragement for both Debbie and her daughter to get used to this new system—and accountability in our counseling sessions—but soon softside Debbie was pointing to the consequences they'd written down instead of pulling out her hair. By breaking her hardside request into small steps, she was able to solve the problem with her feelings—and their relationship—intact.

9. Strengthen your spiritual confidence.

In the next chapter, we'll talk about the tremendous benefits of modeling our love after that of our Savior. Yet we want to make it clear in this chapter that being confident of what God has said in His Word is a powerful aid in expressing love's hard side.

Remember Steve, the golden retriever father whose story began our look at adding hardside love? What gave him the strength to be lovingly tough with his daughter was the confidence that what he was doing was right in God's eyes.

The more clearly we understand our God and His purpose for our lives, the easier it will be to provide whichever side of love our families need. Put another way, the more secure and satisfied we are with Christ as our provider and source of life, the stronger we can be in helping others be all God wants for them.

Where do we get such a confidence level? By studying the Scriptures first, and then any number of devotional and thought-provoking books that can help us deepen our spiritual walk. We especially like the work of authors such as Max Lucado, Ken Gire and Charles Swindoll.[4]

We've now seen nine ways of adding a healthy hardness to our love:

1. Spot emotional freeze points from the past.
2. Allow a short time of distance to build a season of closeness.
3. Learn to say no.
4. Confront what's at the heart of procrastination.
5. Avoid the trap of relying on instant change.
6. Become accountable in love.
7. Build relational bridges to carry hardside words.
8. Break hardside love into steps.
9. Build spiritual confidence.

All are important. And all lead to the tenth.

10. Set a lifetime goal of giving hardside love when it's needed.

Is it time you added more of this side of love to your relationships? It's easy to think of a hundred reasons why you shouldn't start today. But all those excuses may leave you with an empty life.

A current television commercial shows a close-up of a father talking to his son about the dangers of drugs. Suddenly the father breaks into tears and says, "Only, I didn't know I'd need to tell you all this when you were thirteen." Then the camera pans back and shows that the father is speaking to a grave in a lonely, windswept cemetery.

It's not just the fear of what drugs can do to our children that should prompt us to be lovingly hard with them, however. It's a side of love that needs to be part of all our lives. The writer of Hebrews tells us, "The Lord disciplines those he loves."[5] We need a healthy balance of love's hard and soft sides if we're to reflect the love of our heavenly Father.

By now, you should have a list of things you want to do to make your love more balanced. But you need to realize only one consistent power source can enable you to do those things as the years go by. We'll look at that in the last chapter.

12

The Secret to Wholehearted Love

We'd like to say that loving others wholeheartedly is always easy. Unfortunately, it isn't. Sara learned that firsthand. She had to endure trials that most people will never face. Yet she discovered that even in the midst of incredible obstacles, there's an unending, unchanging power source that can sustain and enrich our love.

Sara was thrilled that the handsome young man was to be her husband. He was strong and energetic. And from the moment she met him, she was captivated. They enjoyed many blessings together in those early years, living in the beautiful countryside near their hometown of Rivas, Nicaragua.

First a son was born to Sara and Jose Angel Melendez. Sara would quietly rock her firstborn on the porch and read her Bible or a novel, enjoying the pleasures and challenges of a growing family. Soon she was pregnant with their second baby, and her heart was filled with an ocean of expectations. In a culture full of "religion," she came from a family that emphasized a personal relationship with Christ.

When early signs of her pregnancy were confused with flu symptoms, her uncle, a local physician, prescribed a new drug from West Germany to ease her discomfort. It was called thalidomide.

Unaware of the drug's drastic side effects, the Melendezes were unprepared for what they saw at the time of delivery. Little Tony, their new baby, was born with no arms.

While the doctors and nurses looked after Tony, his parents retreated to the recovery room, devastated. Sara looked for strength to deal with what had happened, and she found it when her mother arrived. The moment she entered the room, she wiped the tears from her daughter's eyes and said, "This is no time for crying. God has sent us this baby. And God knows what he's doing."

From that moment on, Sara found strength in her mother's faith. Her heart softened toward her new boy, so much so that she could pick him up tenderly and say, "Jose Antonio Melendez Rodriguez, . . . you are a beautiful baby. God has given you so much. You have a wonderful face with dark-brown eyes, a cute little nose, pouty lips, and two tiny, perfect ears. . . . You are almost perfect, Antonio. . . . You have . . . a strong, proud neck, broad shoulders, a wonderful chest. . . . You have all the working parts you need to become a strong, beautiful man. God has great dreams for you, . . . and he and I together will see that all those dreams come true."

As the years went by, Tony would learn the incredible softside love his mother brought to the family. Her constant prayers and supportive words ("Don't worry. God has something wonderful in mind for you. Trust him and he will take care of you.") were the guiding force in his life. But Tony also saw her model hardside love at a time when he and the rest of his family most needed it.

After Tony's birth, his father sacrificed greatly to make sure his son received everything he needed. Part of what he needed was medical attention unavailable in his homeland, so Jose moved the family from the comfortable, almost wealthy life they knew in Nicaragua to a dirty, run-down Los Angeles apartment.

Providing for his family meant trading his well-paying profession for dirty, meager jobs at less than minimum wage. It was always Jose's dream, though, to return to Nicaragua, to the life he knew and the land he loved, and raise his family there. The hope of that return sustained him through the indignities he faced as an immigrant trying to provide for his family. And provide he did.

Tony received every bit of attention and help he

needed: surgery to correct a clubbed foot so he could walk, and the best education and physical therapy Jose could provide. Tony blossomed, developing his skills as an artist, musician, athlete and student. He even learned to play his father's guitar beautifully using his feet.

But as the years wore on, the father's dreams faded. He couldn't stand the thought of never being able to return to Nicaragua, and he couldn't bear up under the personal pressure he was putting on himself. In a vain attempt at escape, he started drinking.

By the time Tony was a teenager, alcohol had driven his father into a deteriorating pattern of anger and abuse. The situation was so bad that even their closest family friends suggested Sara take her children and leave. Jose was in a rapid tailspin and refused help, and it looked as if he would destroy the family as he went down.

Yet when times got tough, Sara drew on the hard side of love, which is consistent, determined and disciplined. Of his mother's dedication to his father, Tony would later write, "She refused to abandon the man she loved." She told Tony, "[H]e gave up everything he wanted for his own life in hopes of making our lives better. . . . He struggled against his illness, but it conquered him; and in his time of weakness I just couldn't walk away."

Jose Melendez died on May 24, 1983, of cirrhosis of the liver. He was an alcoholic, but he wasn't abandoned. His family was still together, and his son was still accomplishing things no one could have dreamed. In fact, Tony Melendez played the guitar with his feet for Pope John Paul II during the Pope's 1987 North American tour.[1]

Why Aren't Self-Help Books Ever Enough?

Where does love like Sara Melendez's come from? You may have seen already that it's going to take some real effort to provide the softness others need from you, or especially to become harder in a healthy way. Can't we just make a simple self-help decision and grab hold of the changes we need? For a short time, perhaps, but not for a lifetime.

Depending on our own power to give the two sides of love is like trying to push a car down the street instead of using its engine. We may be able to go a short distance, but each step further drains our energy and invites frustration.

Is there a better way? The truth is, there's only one way, one source of power to truly change our lives for good and maintain those changes for a lifetime. We begin to find it by focusing on a rugged hill outside a walled city. For on that hill stands the hardest—and softest—thing on earth.

Depending on our own power to give the two sides of love is like trying to push a car down the street instead of using its engine.

On a Hill Far Away

There was a day when both time and eternity met. It happened during six hours on a Friday when the sky darkened, the wind howled, and angels wept. Nearly two thousand years ago, on a barren hilltop called Golgotha, the Son of God was crucified.

Christ's death on the cross was both the hardest and softest event in all of history. The cross represents the harshest judgment of sin—*our sin*—imaginable. Nothing could be harder than when God the Father turned His face away from His only Son and the sinless, spotless Lamb of God was scourged, mocked and nailed to a tree to die in our place.

But the cross is also a picture of the softest of all loves. That love was willing to forgive those who drove in the nails, who spit on Him and hit Him with sticks, and who refused to admit that they were killing the rightful King and Lord of glory. That love is the most important thing we'll ever know or experience.

Sara Melendez knew how to be hardside and softside with those she loved, but her strength to do so came from understanding and experiencing God's love.

A God of Balance, a God of Love

Being balanced between our hard and soft sides means accurately reflecting the character of Christ to the world around us. To do that, we've got to be wholehearted in our love for Him, which gives us the power and perspective we need.

Jesus was once asked, "Teacher, which is the greatest commandment in the Law?"

And He answered, " 'Love the Lord your God with all your heart and with all your soul and with all your mind.' This is the first and greatest commandment. And the second is like it: 'Love your neighbor as yourself.' All the Law and the Prophets hang on these two commandments."[2]

Christ certainly knew what He was doing when He joined those two commandments together. The ability to love others is totally dependent on our ability to love Him. The more completely we love Him, the more balanced and complete our love for others will be.

A Man Who Knew

He was the envy of everyone who knew him. Educated in the best schools, he proved himself a worthy student early in life. Not only was he a brilliant scholar who mastered his studies, but he seemed particularly driven to make his knowledge a real part of his life. While others his age frittered away afternoons on boyhood games, this young student absorbed himself in his books. As the years passed, none of his contemporaries could match his zeal for knowledge.

As if that weren't enough, he also came from one of the finest families around. "Bred of good stock," admirers would say. "A fine boy. He's going to do well." His parents provided him with the best of everything. Unfortunately, they also bred into him an arrogant dislike for those things and people that seemed beneath him.

His self-appointed mission in life became the preservation of the heritage his parents left him. In the city where he lived, there were those who threatened to upend his life and culture with a radical philosophy that swept through the country. With the clever arguments of a skilled lawyer, the young crusader challenged any who held this heretical faith. And if they wouldn't listen to his arguments and deny their faith, he could call on the temple guards and a prison sentence or worse to teach them what was "right."

So strong was this man's conviction that one day, he and a group of associates were traveling to another city just to slap down the leaders of this upstart movement. They raced to arrest them—and ran headlong into a supernatural encounter.

Christ's death on the cross was both the hardest and softest event in all of history.

In a split second of time, the man's entire life changed. In one brilliant flash of light that carried the image and words of the risen Lord, this young persecutor became a servant of the Savior. As they helped the zealot to his feet on that dusty road to

Damascus, he was in for a name change—from Saul to Paul—and a lifelong adventure of learning the secret to balanced, wholehearted love for God and others.

Did Paul have a hard side? Absolutely! Of his former life as a persecutor of the church, Luke wrote, "But Saul began to destroy the church. Going from house to house, he dragged off men and women and put them in prison."[3]

But his years in the ministry, like hot steel in a furnace, bent his hard side back into balance. By coming to know God's character and learning how to love people, Paul learned when and how to be hard. And he had many opportunities to apply what he'd learned.

The Corinthian church was a real heartache for Paul. He poured everything he had into the people's lives, and they still lost themselves in divisive arguments, lawsuits against each other, drunkenness at the Lord's table, and tolerating perverted sexual sin in their midst.

Paul was so concerned for their well-being that he planned a personal visit to help straighten them out. First, however, he sent Timothy to try to bring the Corinthians to their senses. He didn't want to be hardside during his visit, but he was prepared to do that if that was best for them.

"Some of you have become arrogant, as if I were not coming to you," he wrote. "But I will come to you very soon, if the Lord is willing, and then I will find out not only how these arrogant people are talking, but what power they have. For the kingdom of God is not a matter of talk but of power. What do you prefer? Shall I come to you with a whip, or in love and with a gentle spirit?"[4]

Paul knew that if he wanted to do what was best for the Corinthians, he had to be willing to rebuke them for their unwillingness to follow Christ's example and teaching. He also knew he wouldn't win any friends doing that, but he was more interested in their relationship with God than he was in winning a popularity contest. He understood hardside love is often the best tool for dealing with sin, and he wasn't afraid to use it.

But God also used the years to breed a gentle softness in Paul. In writing to the Thessalonian church, he once said, "You know we never used flattery, nor did we put on a mask to cover up greed. . . . We were not looking for praise from men. . . . [B]ut we were gentle among you, like a mother caring for her little children."[5] Paul knew the value of tender, compassionate, understanding love. And he knew that one of its values is in encouraging the faith of people who have a sincere love for God.

Where's the Power?

Anyone who has witnessed the launch of the space shuttle knows it's one of the most awesome displays of power you can see. Perched on the launch pad, the shuttle stands eleven stories high and weighs 4.5 million pounds. As the sun creeps over the horizon and splashes its rays across the brilliant blue of an early Florida morning, the shuttle waits there like a silent, white eagle, ready to spring into the heavens.

As the countdown nears, the air grows thick with excitement. Systems are checked and rechecked. More than 143,000 gallons of liquid oxygen, chilled to minus 147 degrees Celsius, have been loaded into the giant external fuel tank. Then mission control gives the go-ahead for the final countdown: "Five, four, three, two, one, SRB ignition!"

For three seconds, 6.5 million pounds of thrust —roughly one-fourth the energy blast that leveled Hiroshima—heave against the combined weight of the shuttle and its tanks and boosters. Then the ivory bird seems to leap off the pad and streak into the sky. It's a sight that is the twentieth century's very definition of power.

For all the genius and technology that go into making the space shuttle, however, it's nothing but a whitewashed can of circuits and microchips without fuel to drive it into space. All that hardware means nothing if there's no power to make it work.

The same thing is true in being balanced with our hard and soft sides. We've come full circle, in a sense, and now we have the information we need to be more wholehearted in our love. But without the power to make it work, all you've got in your hands right now is kindling.

Where does that power come from? From God's Spirit as He takes up residence in our lives when we come to know Christ as Savior. "For God so loved the world [softside] that he gave his one and only Son [hardside], that whoever believes in him shall not perish [hardside] but have eternal life [softside]."[6]

Without God's power found in a personal relationship, a biblical hero like Abraham was a wandering nomad with no future and no family; Moses was a runaway slave with a speech impediment; Samson was another youth hooked on girls and lifting weights; David was another monarch with a wandering eye and no hope for forgiveness; Peter was a mixed-up fisherman who didn't know when to quit; Paul was a radical Pharisee who went off the deep end; and John was a lonely, forgotten old man with crazy dreams.

Making It Work

God's power, found only in that personal relationship with Jesus Christ, makes all the difference. But how do we apply that power in our everyday relationships? What steps can we take to make it active in our lives? We'd like to offer some practical suggestions.

First, admit you need it. Ted Turner was recently quoted as saying, "Christianity is a religion for losers. I don't need anybody to die for me."[7] But while that man may talk tough this side of his day of judgment, he *does* need the Savior, and so do we.

Have you ever acknowledged before God that you can't love others the way you should on your own? Even more important, have you admitted to Him that you can't love Him as you should? Each of us faces God's hard side, but He invites us to accept His soft side of never ending life with Him.

George Toles is a close friend who helped us in many ways with this book. One of his insights speaks right to this point: Our relationship with God always *begins* with having to face His hard side. Think about it. If we recognize that God judges wrong and that we fall far short of His mark of perfection, we're all faced with judgment. But it is precisely His judging, hardside love that points us, urges us, toward His soft side—the way of escape—our Savior, Jesus Christ.

If you've never admitted your need for the Savior and asked Jesus to come into your life, we invite you to do so. Right now, in the quiet of your heart, you can let Jesus into your life and experience a love that is perfect and redemptive. To do that is to invite in all of God's softside love and to know for certain that His hard side will be exercised only in discipline, not judgment.

Simply go to God in prayer; you can use this as your prayer if you'd like: *Dear Lord, I know I've missed the mark in so many ways. I confess that I've looked at pictures of You on the cross all my life but never understood it was me You died for. I know I deserve only the hard side of Your love for all my sins, but I thank You for the softest, warmest love of all that forgives me and gave Your Son to die for me.*

Lord, I don't want to keep You at arm's length anymore. I humbly ask that You come into my life, cleanse my heart from sin, and live in my heart always as my Lord, my shepherd and my lifelong friend. Jesus, each day and in all my relationships, help me learn to walk worthy of Your high calling and great love. Amen.

Even after accepting Christ as Savior, however, we may still not experience the power of His Holy Spirit. Why? There's nothing wrong with God's ability to give us His power, but there's often something that causes us to reject or weaken it. Our culture makes that easy to do.

We live in a world that knows little of God and the power He provides through His Spirit. News reports don't begin with stories of how God's power sustained Christians in the latest catastrophe. Headlines don't read, "God's Power Revealed in Latest Congressional Session." No one talks about it, and few are even aware it's there. But it's the one thing we *must* have to be wholehearted in our love.

Christ told His disciples, "I am the vine; you are the branches. If a man remains in me and I in him, he will bear much fruit; apart from me you can do nothing."[8] Without God's power through abiding in His Spirit, we simply can't make the changes needed to be more balanced in our love. That includes maintaining our time in His Word, prayer, and with His people.

Second, confess your inability to live up to God's standards so you can maintain an open relationship with Him. The Bible calls that human inability *sin,* and sin has a way of clouding our vision and distorting our perception of God. Have you ever had a fight with your spouse and then tried to have a meaningful time with God? It doesn't work well, does it? Anger, guilt and sin act like hardening agents to a loving heart, and they also block a fellowship with the Lord.

Paul told the Ephesians, "'In your anger do not sin': Do not let the sun go down while you are still angry, and do not give the devil a foothold."[9] He understood that anger can harden into sin and weaken all our relationships.

It's not popular today to tell people that sin offends God, but it does. Like anger in a marriage, it drives a wedge between us, and between us and God. When we refuse to deal with wrong in our lives, we create an unhealthy distance in both our human and divine relationships. But confessing our sin or admitting how weak we are on our own clears the air with Him and allows us to develop the fellowship we must have to abide in Him, live in His power and genuinely love others.

Finally, take a step of faith, and trust God for the power to change. In seminars and counseling all across the country, we're often asked, "What do I do if I don't love my spouse anymore?" The answer is to *first put love into action, and wait for the feelings to follow.* In other words, don't wait until your feelings change for the better before you do something; take the right kind of action, and eventually your feelings will catch up with your loving deeds.

If you're a golden retriever or otter who needs to add some hardside characteristics, or if you're a lion or beaver who needs to develop a healthy softness, don't wait until you feel God's power and then try to change. There's no faith involved in that. *Start making the right changes, and trust God to supply the power as you need it.*

Corrie ten Boom used to tell how her father taught her what faith means. "When you go to the train station, do you buy your ticket before you get there or after?" he asked.

"After, Papa," she answered.

"In the same way," he explained, "God gives you the faith you need to face life *at the moment you need it,* not before."

The writer to the Hebrews tells us, "And without faith it is impossible to please God, because anyone who comes to him must believe that he exists and that he rewards those who earnestly seek him."[10] If we seek God wholeheartedly and trust Him enough to begin instituting changes, He will faithfully reward us with the power to make those changes a reality.

We've come to the end of our look at the two

sides of love. Our prayer for you is that in the days to come, you'll discover more of God's love than ever before.

May you always be humbled by the hardness of love pictured in the cross, and thankful for His discipline when we need it. And may you also be thankful for the softness that sent God's only begotten Son to that cross—and would have done so even if you had been the only one without hope otherwise.

May the Lord bless you and keep you. May you come to know Him as both your mighty king and loving shepherd. And may all your relationships express what Jesus gave to others, the two sides of love.

Notes

Chapter 1

1. In Hebrew, the original language of the Old Testament, there's a very close grammatical and personal connection between the two figures of speech in this passage. Normally, two circumstantial clauses, like those found in Isaiah 40:10-11, would be connected by a Waw consecutive (similar to an English *and*). However, so close is the connection in this case that no conjunction exists between the two clauses.

   In short, the "Sovereign Lord" (*Adonai Jehovah* in Hebrew) who comes in strength is directly linked with the picture of a compassionate shepherd. His "power" with which "his arm rules for him" cannot be separated from the great love out of which he "gathers the lambs in his arms" and "gently leads those that have young."

   For further insight into these powerful figures of speech, see C. F. Keil and F. Delitzsch, *Commentary on the Old Testament in Ten Volumes*, vol. 7, *Isaiah* (Grand Rapids, Mich.: Eerdmans, 1975), pp. 145-47; Edward J. Young, *The Book of Isaiah*, vol. 3 (Grand Rapids, Mich.: Eerdmans, 1972), pp. 38-40; E. Kautzsch, *Genenius' Hebrew Grammar*, rev. ed. (London: Oxford U., 1974), pp. 504-5.

2. Romans 5:8.

3. Matthew 16:17.
4. Matthew 16:23.
5. Luke 9:51.

Chapter 3

1. Ross Campbell, *How to Really Love Your Child* (Wheaton, Ill.: Victor, 1978), pp. 14–16.
2. For those who want to go deeper in understanding their personality, a number of popular tests are available, including the *Myers-Briggs* test, the *Keirsey Temperament Sorter* and the *Taylor-Johnson Temperament Analysis*. Our friend Florence Littauer has also written a helpful book called *Personality Plus*.

   As mentioned in the chapter, we strongly recommend Dr. Williamson's *"Pro Scan" PDP Personality Survey* as well. After taking it, you get back an exhaustive, ten-page analysis that helps you identify your stress and energy levels, how you make decisions, how best to motivate yourself and others, and so on. For further information, write to Dr. Michael Williamson, CompuLink, 408 S. Santa Anita Ave., #13, Arcadia, CA 91006. To order the test, call 800-332-3291. The call is toll-free, but there is a reasonable fee for the ten-page analysis.

   Another helpful test is the *Couple's Profile* developed by the Reverend Charles Boyd in conjunction with Performax International. It gives engaged and married *couples* a good look at themselves and their differences and is used extensively in Campus Crusade's Family Life Conferences. For more information, write to Boyd at #3 Diamond Pointe Cove, Maumelle, AR 72113. To order, send $12 per profile plus $3 shipping and handling. Specify whether you want the *engaged* or *married* version.

   Yet another helpful test is the *Personal Style Indicator,* which is slanted primarily toward business use but offers strong insights and applications for a family as well. For more details, write to Terry Anderson, Consulting Resource Group International, #386-

33255 S. Fraser Way, Abbotsford, B.C., Canada V2S 2B2 or #386-200 W. Third St., Sumas, WA 98295-8000.

Chapter 4

1. Ross Campbell, *How to Really Love Your Child,* pp. 14–16.
2. For an in-depth treatment of the concept of closing a person's spirit, see Gary Smalley, *The Key to Your Child's Heart* (Waco, Tex.: Word, 1984). Look especially at chapter 1, "How to Overcome the Major Destroyer of Families."

Chapter 5

1. An excellent new book on establishing discipline and responsibility with our kids is *Who's in Charge Here?*, by Robert G. Barnes, Jr. (Dallas: Word, 1990).
2. Hebrews 11:1.

Chapter 6

1. For the heroic, inspiring account of what it was like to be a prisoner of war in North Vietnam for eight and a half years, see Everett Alvarez, Jr., *Chained Eagle* (New York: Donald I. Fine, 1989).
2. 1 Samuel 16:7.
3. C. F. Keil and F. Delitzsch, *Commentary on the Old Testament in Ten Volumes,* vol. 2, *Joshua, Judges, Ruth, I & II Samuel* (Grand Rapids, Mich.: Eerdmans, 1975), pp. 153–59.
4. An excellent book on peer pressure is Joe White's *Friendship Pressure* (Sisters, Ore.: Questar, 1989).

Chapter 7

1. Leonard Maltin, *The Disney Films,* rev. ed. (New York: Crown, 1984), section on *Greyfriar's Bobby.*
2. For information about how to bring the "Love Is a

Decision" seminar to your city, write to Terry Brown or Norma Smalley at Today's Family, P.O. Box 22111, Phoenix, AZ 85028.
3. For a good perspective on this common problem, see Robert Hemfelt, Paul Meier and Frank Minirth, *Love Is a Choice* (Nashville: Nelson, 1989).
4. *World Book Encyclopedia* (Chicago: World Book, 1988), pp. 570–71.

Chapter 8

1. There are many good books that will help you deal with a hurtful past. Here are just a few we recommend: our own books *The Blessing* and *The Gift of Honor* (both from Thomas Nelson); *Healing for Damaged Emotions,* by David Seamands (Victor); *Unfinished Business: Helping Adult Children Resolve Their Past,* by Charles Sell (Multnomah); *The Missing Piece,* by Lee Ezell (Harvest House); *Unlocking the Secrets of Your Childhood Memories,* by Kevin Leman and Randy Carlson (Thomas Nelson).
2. See Richard B. Stuart, *Helping Couples Change* (New York: Guilford, 1980), especially "Caring Days: A technique for building commitment to faltering marriages," pp. 192–208.

Chapter 9

1. Matthew 6:21.
2. Proverbs 15:1; 25:15.
3. *The Student Bible* (Grand Rapids, Mich.: Zondervan, 1986).
4. See James 1:23–25.
5. Proverbs 15:30.
6. Proverbs 17:10, *New American Standard Bible.*
7. Psalm 44:20–21.
8. To get a copy of this important book, you can contact Jim Brawner directly at HCR4, Box 2212-A, Branson, MO 65616.

Chapter 10

1. John 8:32.

Chapter 11

1. Acts 24:25.
2. Proverbs 27:17.
3. Proverbs 27:6, *New American Standard Bible*.
4. Some of our favorite books by these authors are: Max Lucado, *No Wonder They Call Him Savior* and *Six Hours One Friday* (both from Multnomah); Ken Gire, *Intimate Moments with the Savior* (Zondervan); Charles Swindoll, *Come Before Winter, Rise & Shine* (both from Multnomah) and *The Grace Awakening* (Word).
5. Hebrews 12:6.

Chapter 12

1. Tony Melendez with Mel White, *A Gift of Hope* (San Francisco: Harper & Row, 1989), pp. 17, 19, 147–48.
2. Matthew 22:37–40.
3. Acts 8:3.
4. 1 Corinthians 4:18–21.
5. 1 Thessalonians 2:5–7.
6. John 3:16.
7. *Youthworker Update*, vol. iv, no. 5, January 1990, p. 8.
8. John 15:5.
9. Ephesians 4:26–27.
10. Hebrews 11:6.